D1196107

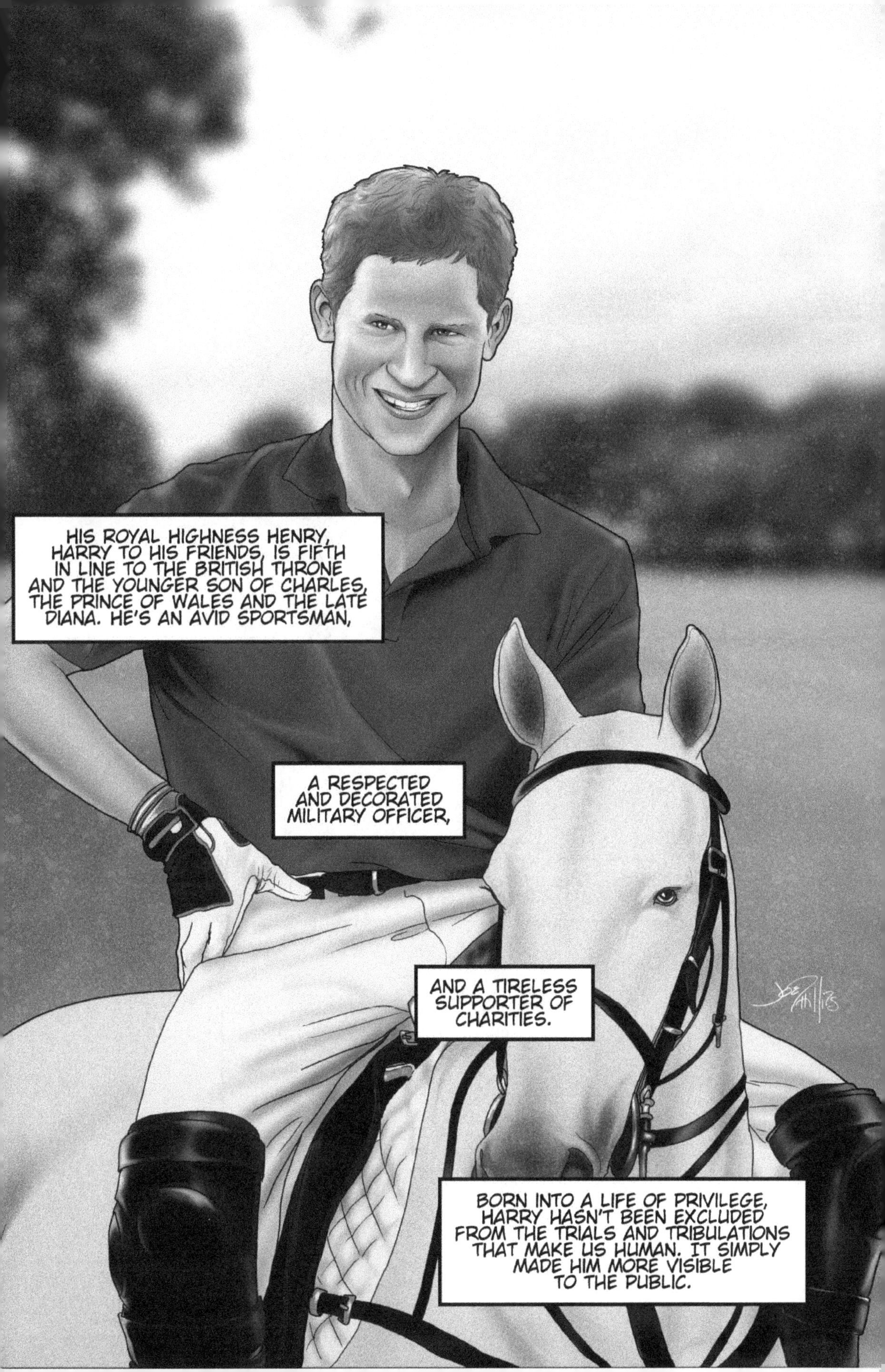
HIS ROYAL HIGHNESS HENRY, HARRY TO HIS FRIENDS, IS FIFTH IN LINE TO THE BRITISH THRONE AND THE YOUNGER SON OF CHARLES, THE PRINCE OF WALES AND THE LATE DIANA. HE'S AN AVID SPORTSMAN,
A RESPECTED AND DECORATED MILITARY OFFICER,
AND A TIRELESS SUPPORTER OF CHARITIES.
BORN INTO A LIFE OF PRIVILEGE, HARRY HASN'T BEEN EXCLUDED FROM THE TRIALS AND TRIBULATIONS THAT MAKE US HUMAN. IT SIMPLY MADE HIM MORE VISIBLE TO THE PUBLIC.

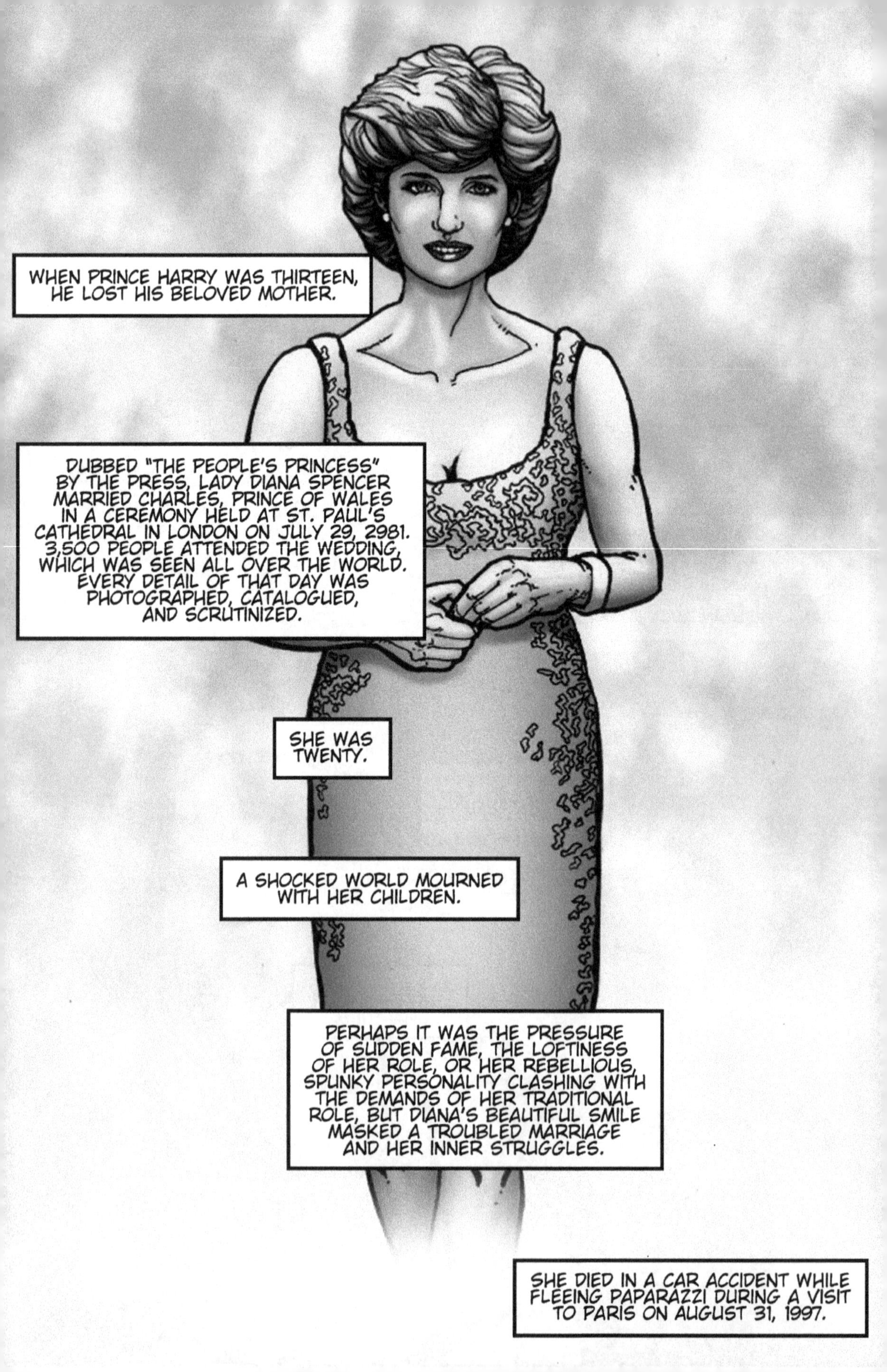
WHEN PRINCE HARRY WAS THIRTEEN, HE LOST HIS BELOVED MOTHER.
DUBBED "THE PEOPLE'S PRINCESS" BY THE PRESS, LADY DIANA SPENCER MARRIED CHARLES, PRINCE OF WALES IN A CEREMONY HELD AT ST. PAUL'S CATHEDRAL IN LONDON ON JULY 29, 2981. 3,500 PEOPLE ATTENDED THE WEDDING, WHICH WAS SEEN ALL OVER THE WORLD. EVERY DETAIL OF THAT DAY WAS PHOTOGRAPHED, CATALOGUED, AND SCRUTINIZED.
SHE WAS TWENTY.
A SHOCKED WORLD MOURNED WITH HER CHILDREN.
PERHAPS IT WAS THE PRESSURE OF SUDDEN FAME, THE LOFTINESS OF HER ROLE, OR HER REBELLIOUS, SPUNKY PERSONALITY CLASHING WITH THE DEMANDS OF HER TRADITIONAL ROLE, BUT DIANA'S BEAUTIFUL SMILE MASKED A TROUBLED MARRIAGE AND HER INNER STRUGGLES.
SHE DIED IN A CAR ACCIDENT WHILE FLEEING PAPARAZZI DURING A VISIT TO PARIS ON AUGUST 31, 1997.

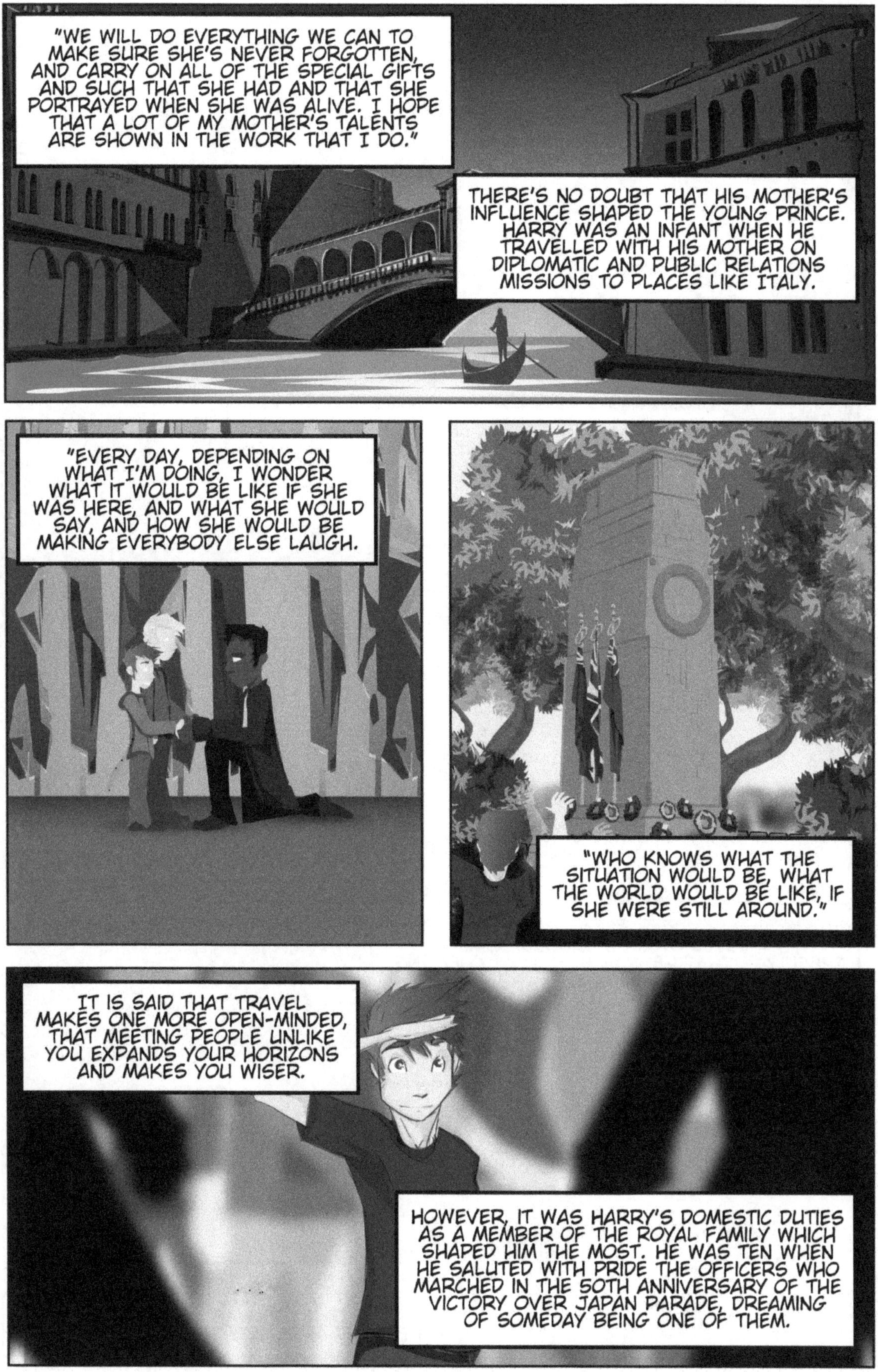
"WE WILL DO EVERYTHING WE CAN TO MAKE SURE SHE'S NEVER FORGOTTEN, AND CARRY ON ALL OF THE SPECIAL GIFTS AND SUCH THAT SHE HAD AND THAT SHE PORTRAYED WHEN SHE WAS ALIVE. I HOPE THAT A LOT OF MY MOTHER'S TALENTS ARE SHOWN IN THE WORK THAT I DO."
THERE'S NO DOUBT THAT HIS MOTHER'S INFLUENCE SHAPED THE YOUNG PRINCE. HARRY WAS AN INFANT WHEN HE TRAVELLED WITH HIS MOTHER ON DIPLOMATIC AND PUBLIC RELATIONS MISSIONS TO PLACES LIKE ITALY.
"EVERY DAY, DEPENDING ON WHAT I'M DOING, I WONDER WHAT IT WOULD BE LIKE IF SHE WAS HERE, AND WHAT SHE WOULD SAY, AND HOW SHE WOULD BE MAKING EVERYBODY ELSE LAUGH.
"WHO KNOWS WHAT THE SITUATION WOULD BE, WHAT THE WORLD WOULD BE LIKE, IF SHE WERE STILL AROUND."
IT IS SAID THAT TRAVEL MAKES ONE MORE OPEN-MINDED, THAT MEETING PEOPLE UNLIKE YOU EXPANDS YOUR HORIZONS AND MAKES YOU WISER.
HOWEVER, IT WAS HARRY'S DOMESTIC DUTIES AS A MEMBER OF THE ROYAL FAMILY WHICH SHAPED HIM THE MOST. HE WAS TEN WHEN HE SALUTED WITH PRIDE THE OFFICERS WHO MARCHED IN THE 50TH ANNIVERSARY OF THE VICTORY OVER JAPAN PARADE, DREAMING OF SOMEDAY BEING ONE OF THEM.

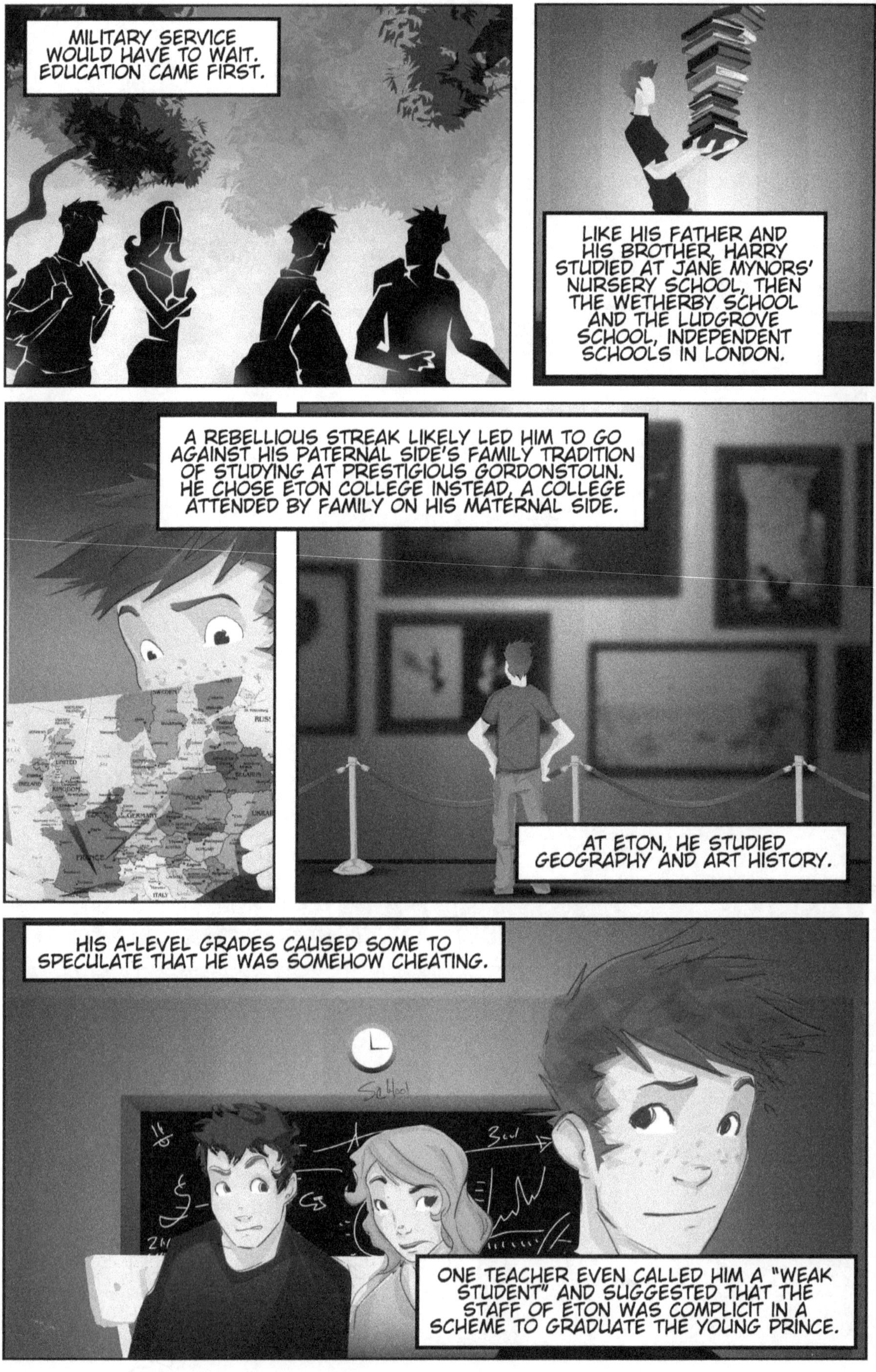
MILITARY SERVICE WOULD HAVE TO WAIT. EDUCATION CAME FIRST.
LIKE HIS FATHER AND HIS BROTHER, HARRY STUDIED AT JANE MYNORS' NURSERY SCHOOL, THEN THE WETHERBY SCHOOL AND THE LUDGROVE SCHOOL, INDEPENDENT SCHOOLS IN LONDON.
A REBELLIOUS STREAK LIKELY LED HIM TO GO AGAINST HIS PATERNAL SIDE'S FAMILY TRADITION OF STUDYING AT PRESTIGIOUS GORDONSTOUN. HE CHOSE ETON COLLEGE INSTEAD, A COLLEGE ATTENDED BY FAMILY ON HIS MATERNAL SIDE.
AT ETON, HE STUDIED GEOGRAPHY AND ART HISTORY.
HIS A-LEVEL GRADES CAUSED SOME TO SPECULATE THAT HE WAS SOMEHOW CHEATING.
ONE TEACHER EVEN CALLED HIM A "WEAK STUDENT" AND SUGGESTED THAT THE STAFF OF ETON WAS COMPLICIT IN A SCHEME TO GRADUATE THE YOUNG PRINCE.

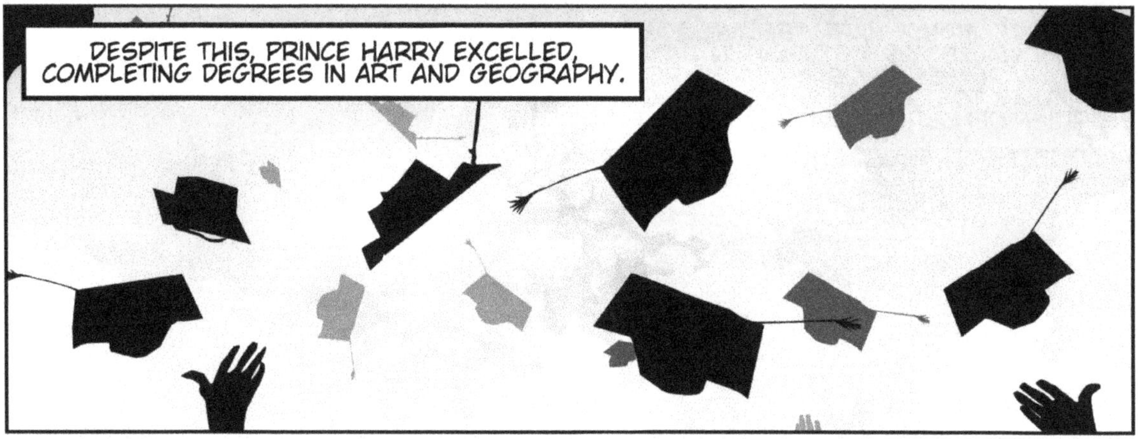
DESPITE THIS, PRINCE HARRY EXCELLED, COMPLETING DEGREES IN ART AND GEOGRAPHY.

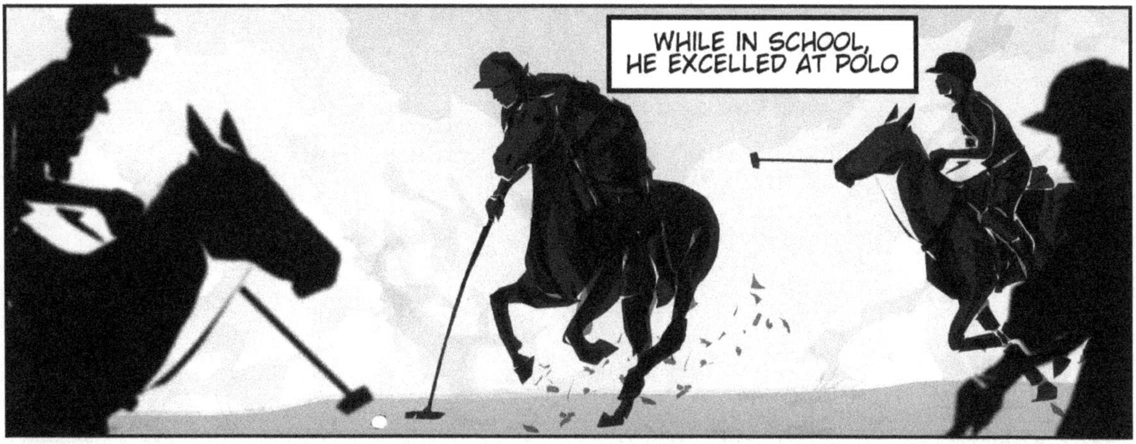
WHILE IN SCHOOL, HE EXCELLED AT POLO

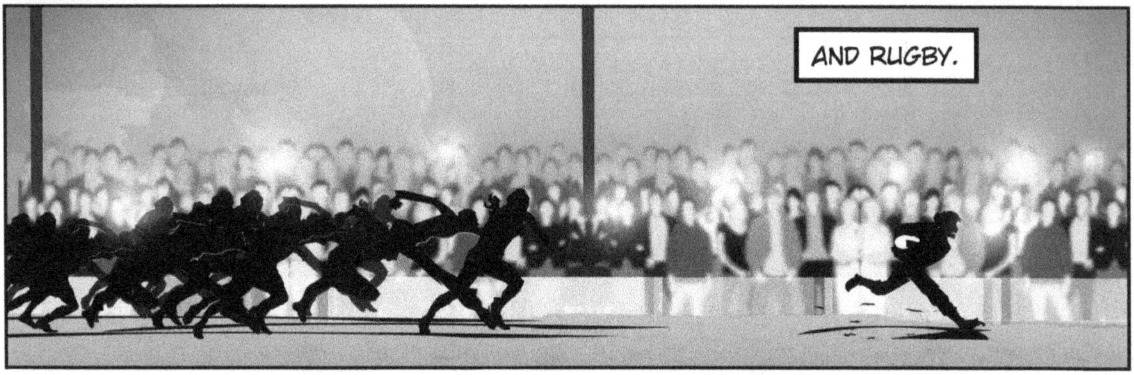
AND RUGBY.

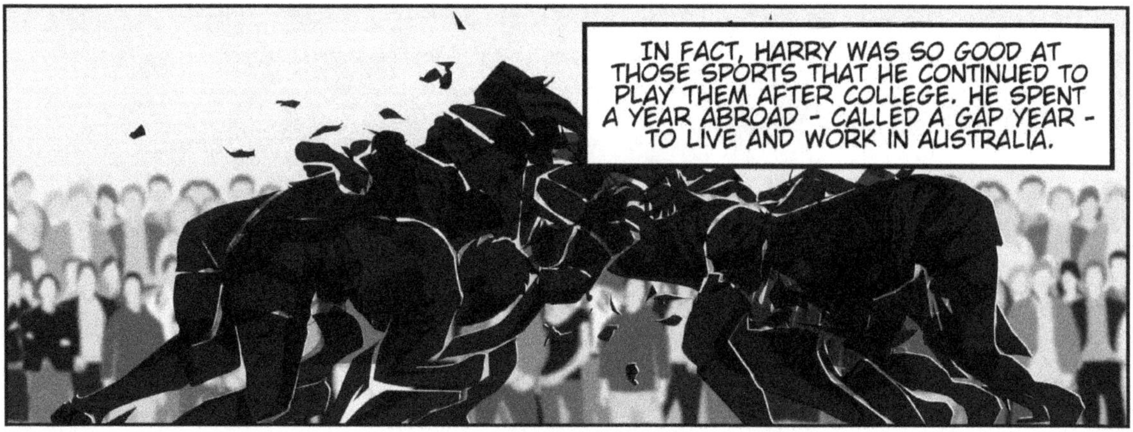
IN FACT, HARRY WAS SO GOOD AT THOSE SPORTS THAT HE CONTINUED TO PLAY THEM AFTER COLLEGE. HE SPENT A YEAR ABROAD - CALLED A GAP YEAR - TO LIVE AND WORK IN AUSTRALIA.

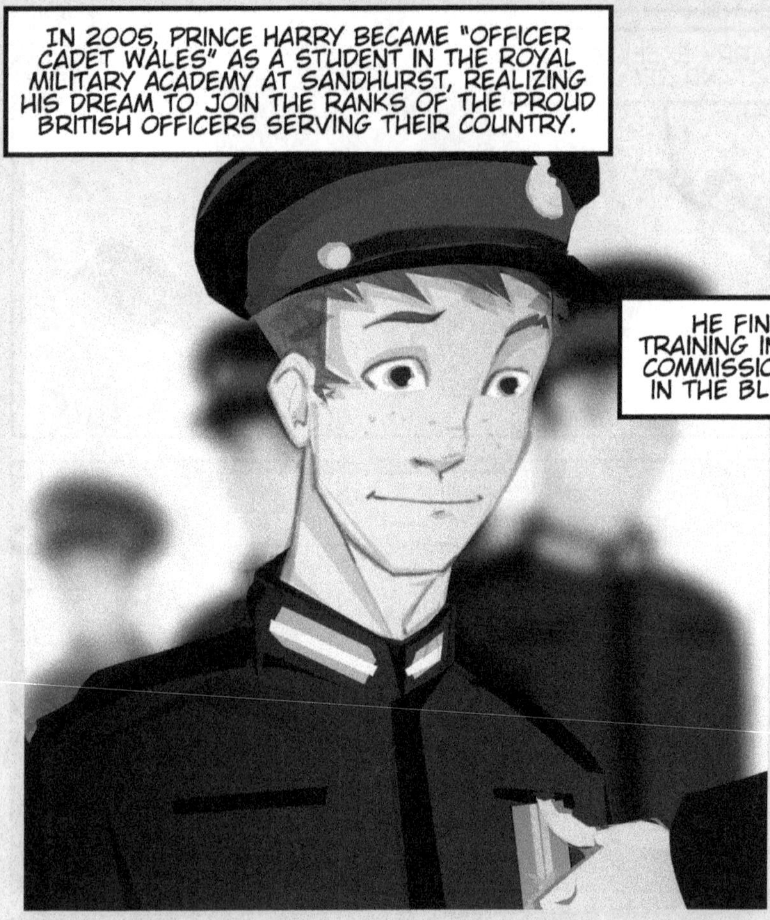
IN 2005, PRINCE HARRY BECAME "OFFICER CADET WALES" AS A STUDENT IN THE ROYAL MILITARY ACADEMY AT SANDHURST, REALIZING HIS DREAM TO JOIN THE RANKS OF THE PROUD BRITISH OFFICERS SERVING THEIR COUNTRY.
HE FINISHED OFFICER TRAINING IN A YEAR AND WAS COMMISSIONED AS A CORNET IN THE BLUES AND ROYALS.

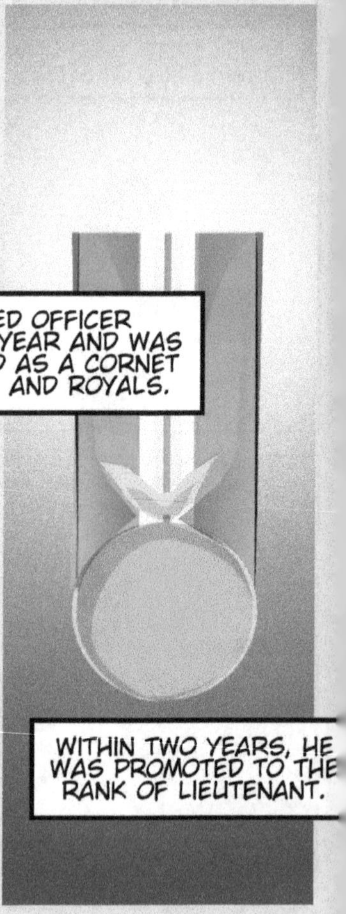
WITHIN TWO YEARS, HE WAS PROMOTED TO THE RANK OF LIEUTENANT.

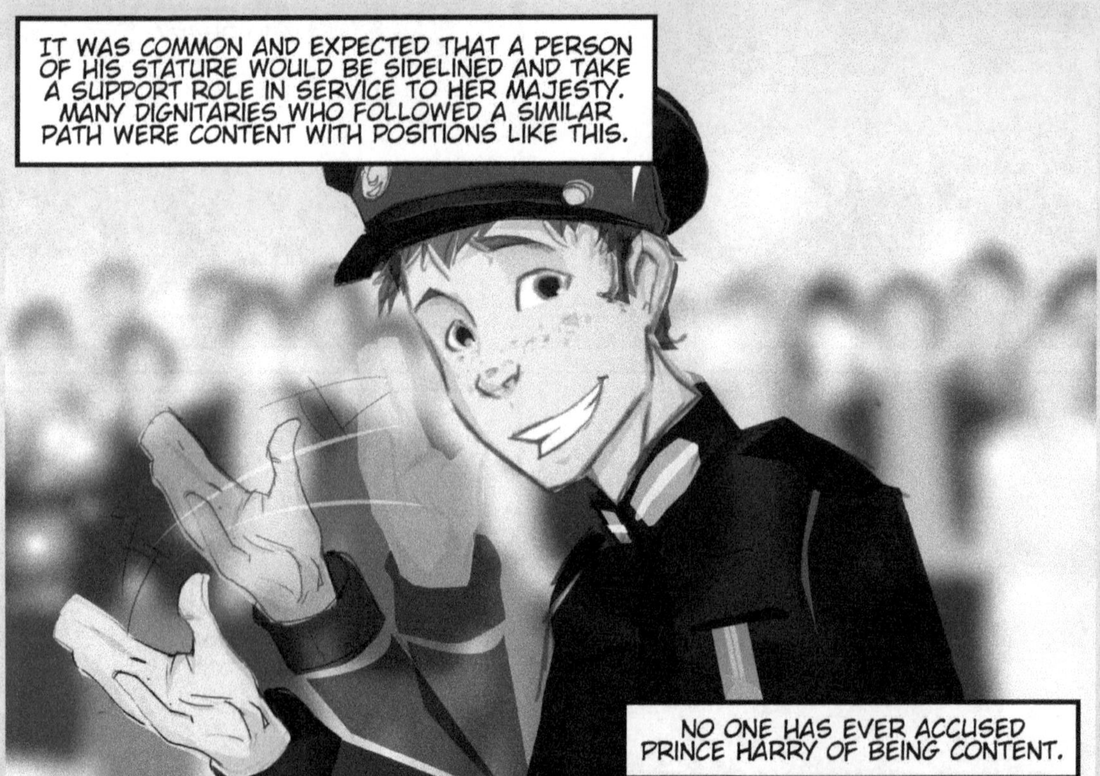
IT WAS COMMON AND EXPECTED THAT A PERSON OF HIS STATURE WOULD BE SIDELINED AND TAKE A SUPPORT ROLE IN SERVICE TO HER MAJESTY. MANY DIGNITARIES WHO FOLLOWED A SIMILAR PATH WERE CONTENT WITH POSITIONS LIKE THIS.
NO ONE HAS EVER ACCUSED PRINCE HARRY OF BEING CONTENT.

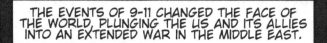

THE EVENTS OF 9-11 CHANGED THE FACE OF THE WORLD, PLUNGING THE US AND ITS ALLIES INTO AN EXTENDED WAR IN THE MIDDLE EAST.

MANY FEARED THAT HARRY WAS TOO HIGH-VALUE AS A TARGET AND, SHOULD HE BECOME INVOLVED PERSONALLY IN THE CONFLICT ON THE GROUND, HE'D BE A DANGER TO ALL IN HIS UNIT, THREATENING HIS DREAM.

THE MEN AND WOMEN HE SERVED WITH THOUGHT OTHERWISE.

SOLDIERS IN HIS UNIT PROUDLY WORE SHIRTS EMBLAZONED WITH THE WORDS "I'M HARRY!" WHILE ON DEPLOYMENT. SHOULD ENEMIES SEEK TO CAPTURE OR KILL THE YOUNG PRINCE, THEY'D HAVE A TOUGH TIME DISCERNING WHO WAS WHO.

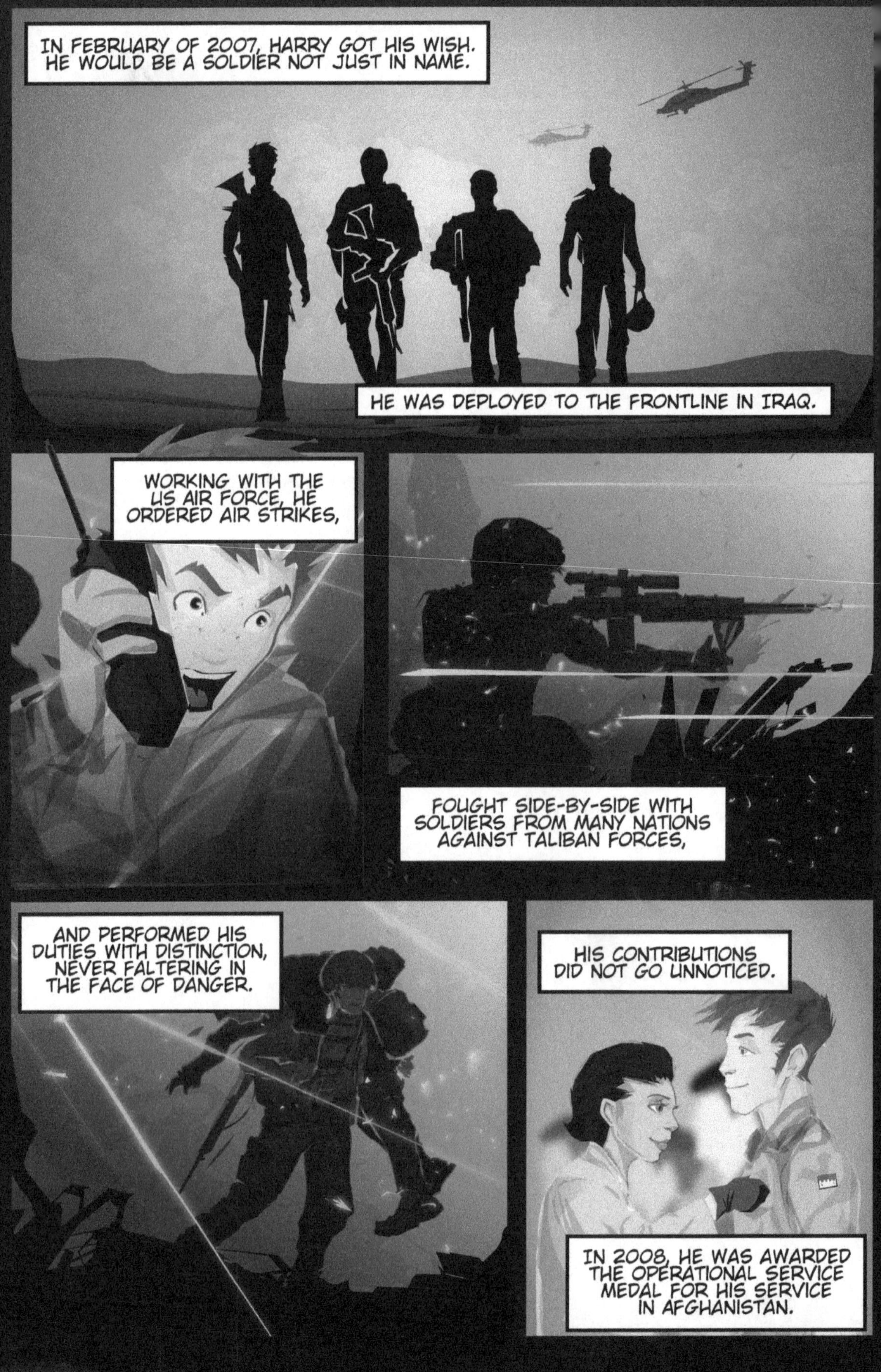
IN FEBRUARY OF 2007, HARRY GOT HIS WISH. HE WOULD BE A SOLDIER NOT JUST IN NAME.
HE WAS DEPLOYED TO THE FRONTLINE IN IRAQ.
WORKING WITH THE US AIR FORCE, HE ORDERED AIR STRIKES,
FOUGHT SIDE-BY-SIDE WITH SOLDIERS FROM MANY NATIONS AGAINST TALIBAN FORCES,
AND PERFORMED HIS DUTIES WITH DISTINCTION, NEVER FALTERING IN THE FACE OF DANGER.
HIS CONTRIBUTIONS DID NOT GO UNNOTICED.
IN 2008, HE WAS AWARDED THE OPERATIONAL SERVICE MEDAL FOR HIS SERVICE IN AFGHANISTAN.

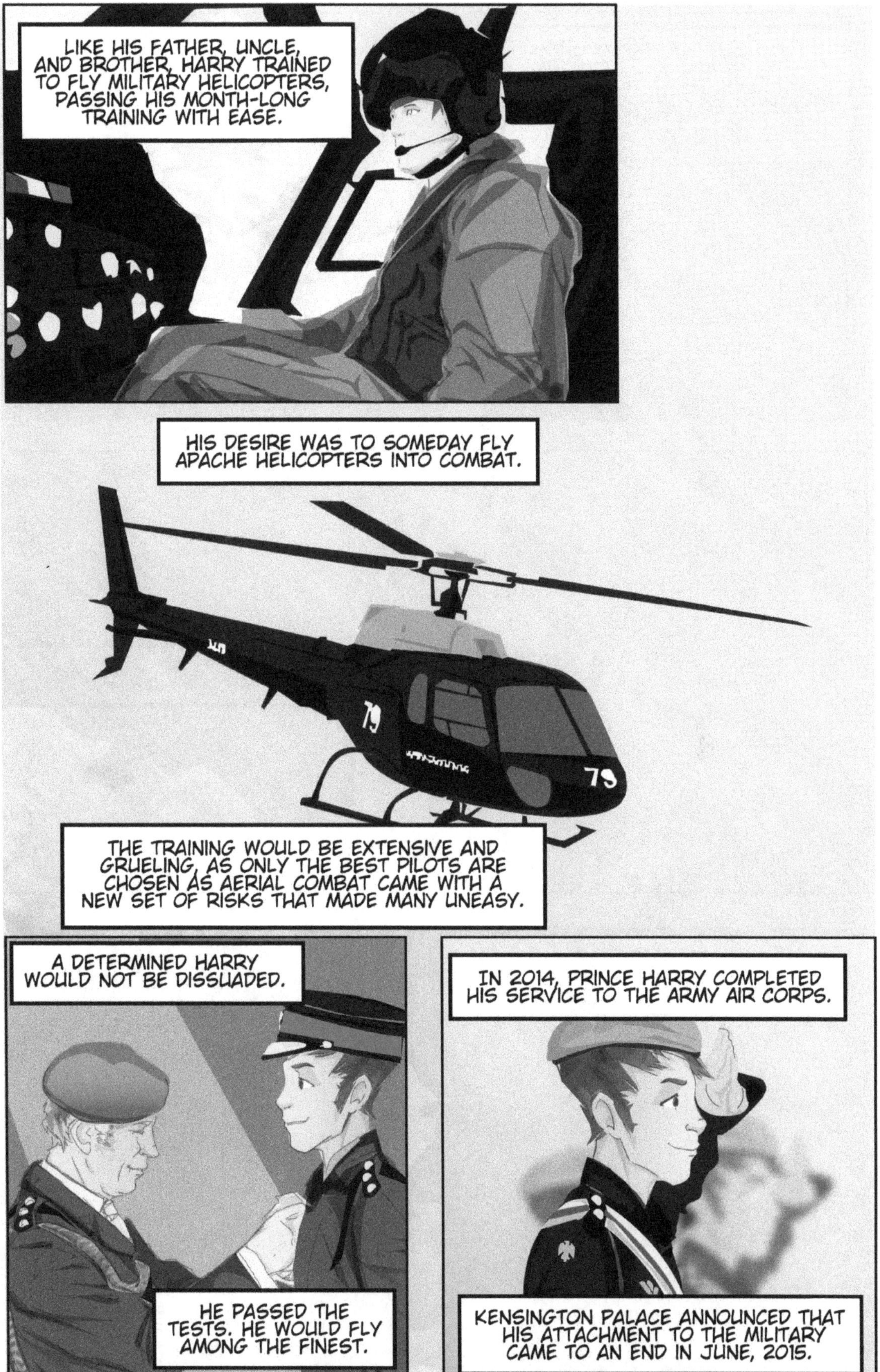
LIKE HIS FATHER, UNCLE, AND BROTHER, HARRY TRAINED TO FLY MILITARY HELICOPTERS, PASSING HIS MONTH-LONG TRAINING WITH EASE.
HIS DESIRE WAS TO SOMEDAY FLY APACHE HELICOPTERS INTO COMBAT.
THE TRAINING WOULD BE EXTENSIVE AND GRUELING, AS ONLY THE BEST PILOTS ARE CHOSEN AS AERIAL COMBAT CAME WITH A NEW SET OF RISKS THAT MADE MANY UNEASY.
A DETERMINED HARRY WOULD NOT BE DISSUADED.
HE PASSED THE TESTS. HE WOULD FLY AMONG THE FINEST.
IN 2014, PRINCE HARRY COMPLETED HIS SERVICE TO THE ARMY AIR CORPS.
KENSINGTON PALACE ANNOUNCED THAT HIS ATTACHMENT TO THE MILITARY CAME TO AN END IN JUNE, 2015.

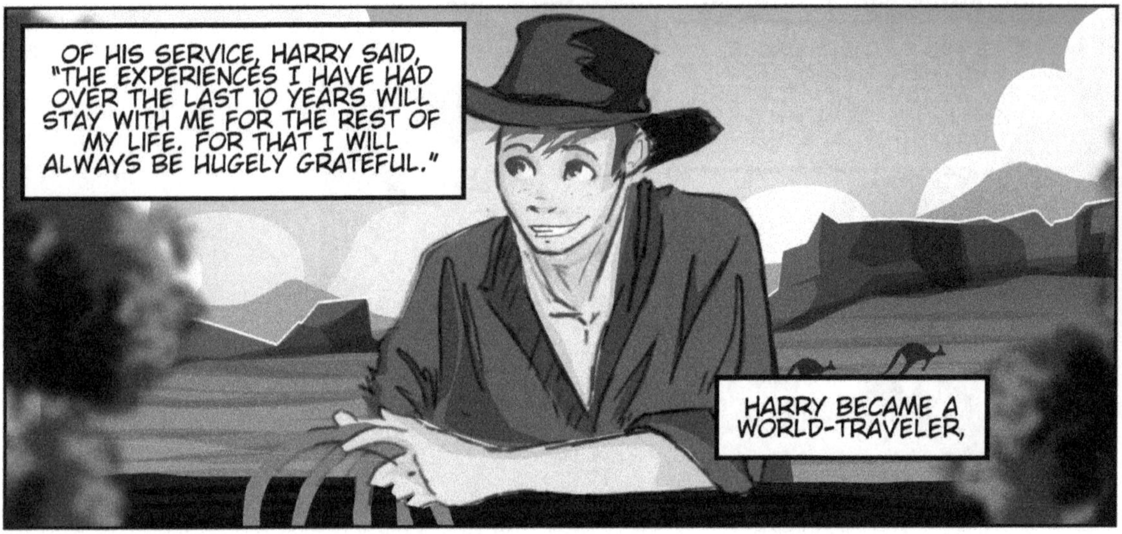
OF HIS SERVICE, HARRY SAID, "THE EXPERIENCES I HAVE HAD OVER THE LAST 10 YEARS WILL STAY WITH ME FOR THE REST OF MY LIFE. FOR THAT I WILL ALWAYS BE HUGELY GRATEFUL."
HARRY BECAME A WORLD-TRAVELER,

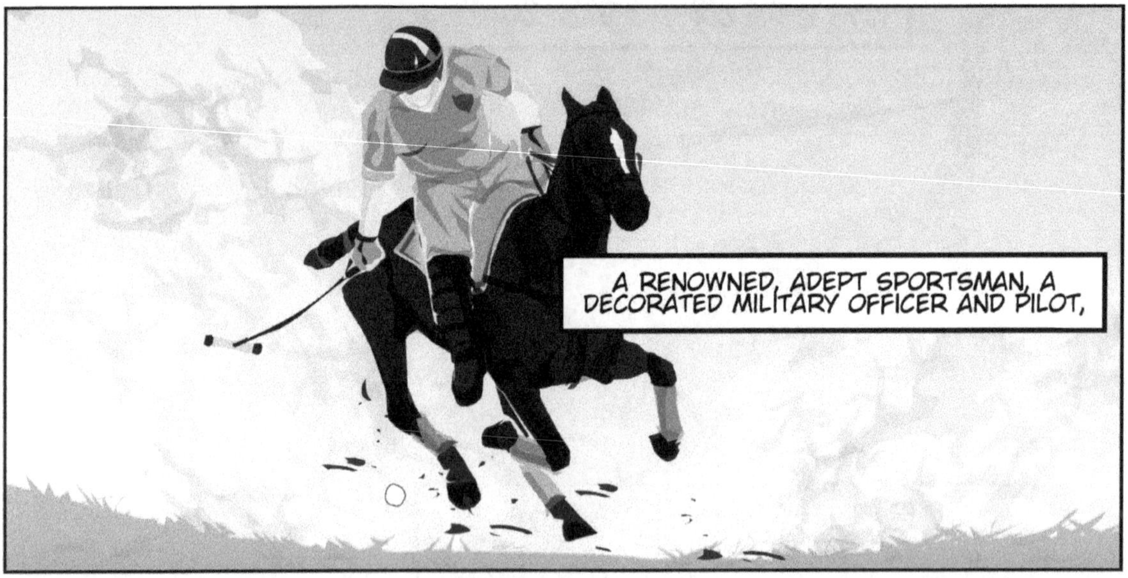
A RENOWNED, ADEPT SPORTSMAN, A DECORATED MILITARY OFFICER AND PILOT,

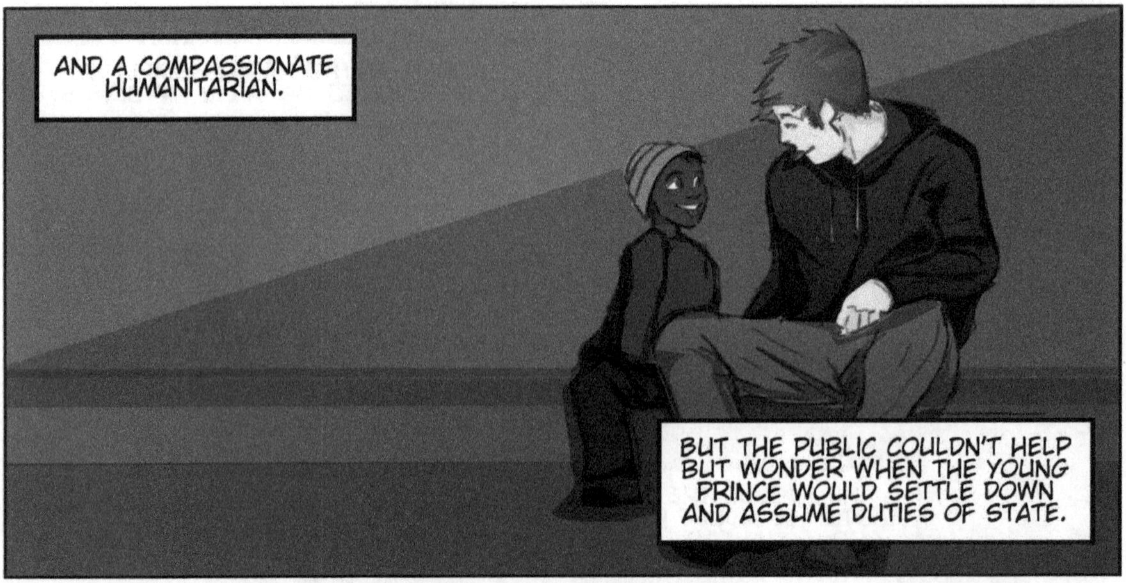
AND A COMPASSIONATE HUMANITARIAN.
BUT THE PUBLIC COULDN'T HELP BUT WONDER WHEN THE YOUNG PRINCE WOULD SETTLE DOWN AND ASSUME DUTIES OF STATE.

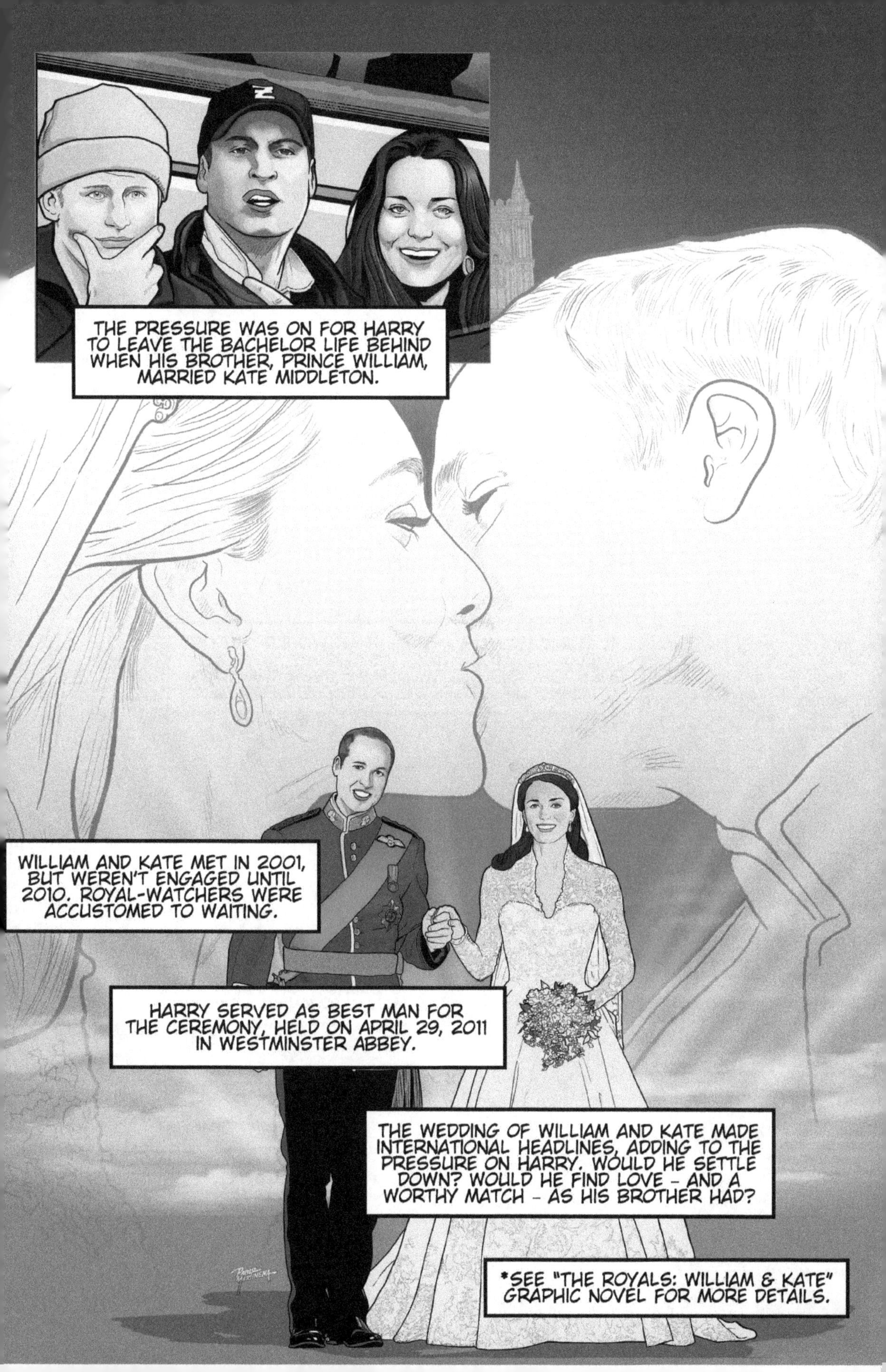
THE PRESSURE WAS ON FOR HARRY TO LEAVE THE BACHELOR LIFE BEHIND WHEN HIS BROTHER, PRINCE WILLIAM, MARRIED KATE MIDDLETON.
WILLIAM AND KATE MET IN 2001, BUT WEREN'T ENGAGED UNTIL 2010. ROYAL-WATCHERS WERE ACCUSTOMED TO WAITING.
HARRY SERVED AS BEST MAN FOR THE CEREMONY, HELD ON APRIL 29, 2011 IN WESTMINSTER ABBEY.
THE WEDDING OF WILLIAM AND KATE MADE INTERNATIONAL HEADLINES, ADDING TO THE PRESSURE ON HARRY. WOULD HE SETTLE DOWN? WOULD HE FIND LOVE - AND A WORTHY MATCH - AS HIS BROTHER HAD?
*SEE "THE ROYALS: WILLIAM & KATE" GRAPHIC NOVEL FOR MORE DETAILS.

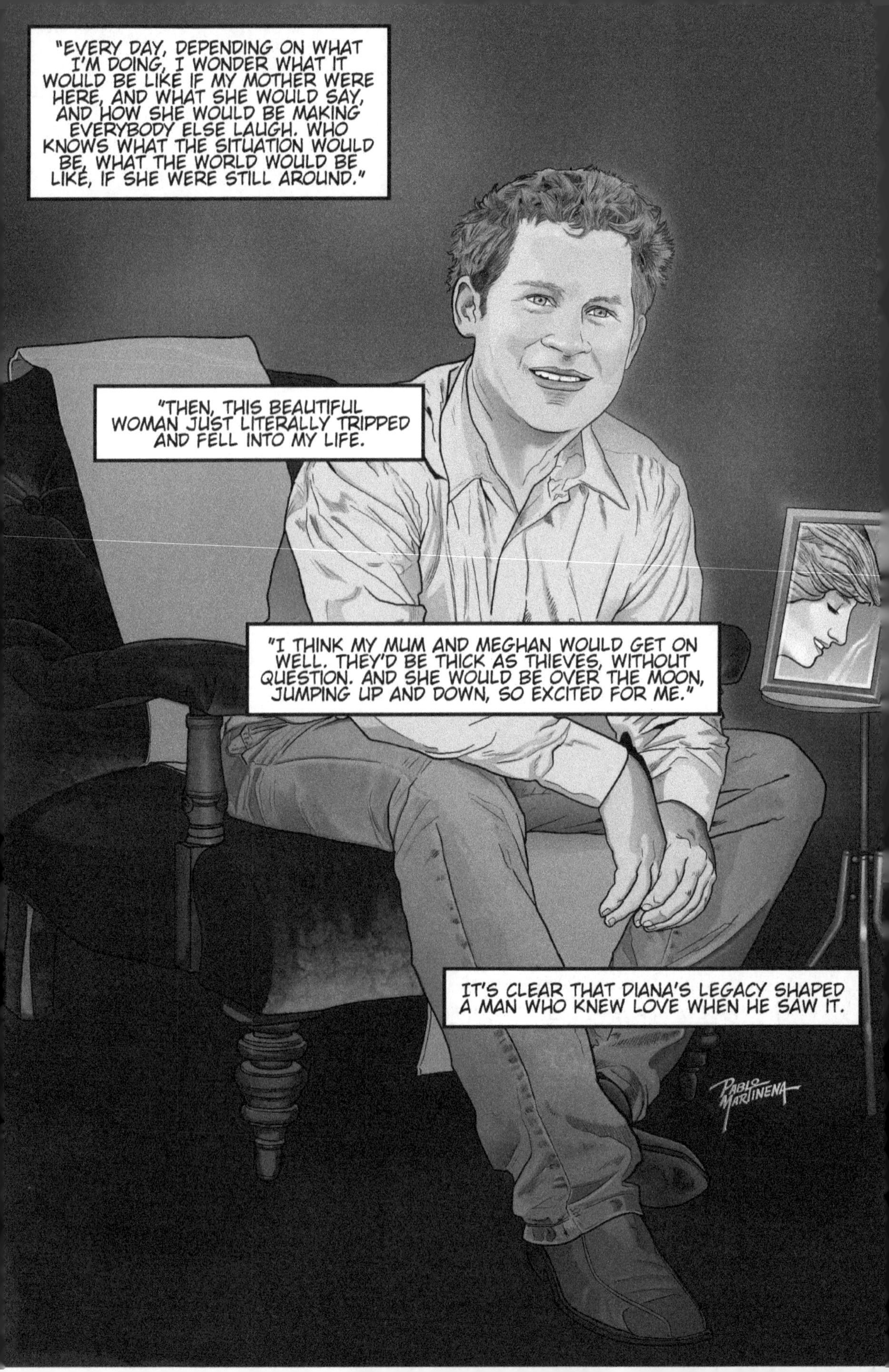
"EVERY DAY, DEPENDING ON WHAT I'M DOING, I WONDER WHAT IT WOULD BE LIKE IF MY MOTHER WERE HERE, AND WHAT SHE WOULD SAY, AND HOW SHE WOULD BE MAKING EVERYBODY ELSE LAUGH. WHO KNOWS WHAT THE SITUATION WOULD BE, WHAT THE WORLD WOULD BE LIKE, IF SHE WERE STILL AROUND."
"THEN, THIS BEAUTIFUL WOMAN JUST LITERALLY TRIPPED AND FELL INTO MY LIFE.
"I THINK MY MUM AND MEGHAN WOULD GET ON WELL. THEY'D BE THICK AS THIEVES, WITHOUT QUESTION. AND SHE WOULD BE OVER THE MOON, JUMPING UP AND DOWN, SO EXCITED FOR ME."
IT'S CLEAR THAT DIANA'S LEGACY SHAPED A MAN WHO KNEW LOVE WHEN HE SAW IT.
PABLO MARTINENA

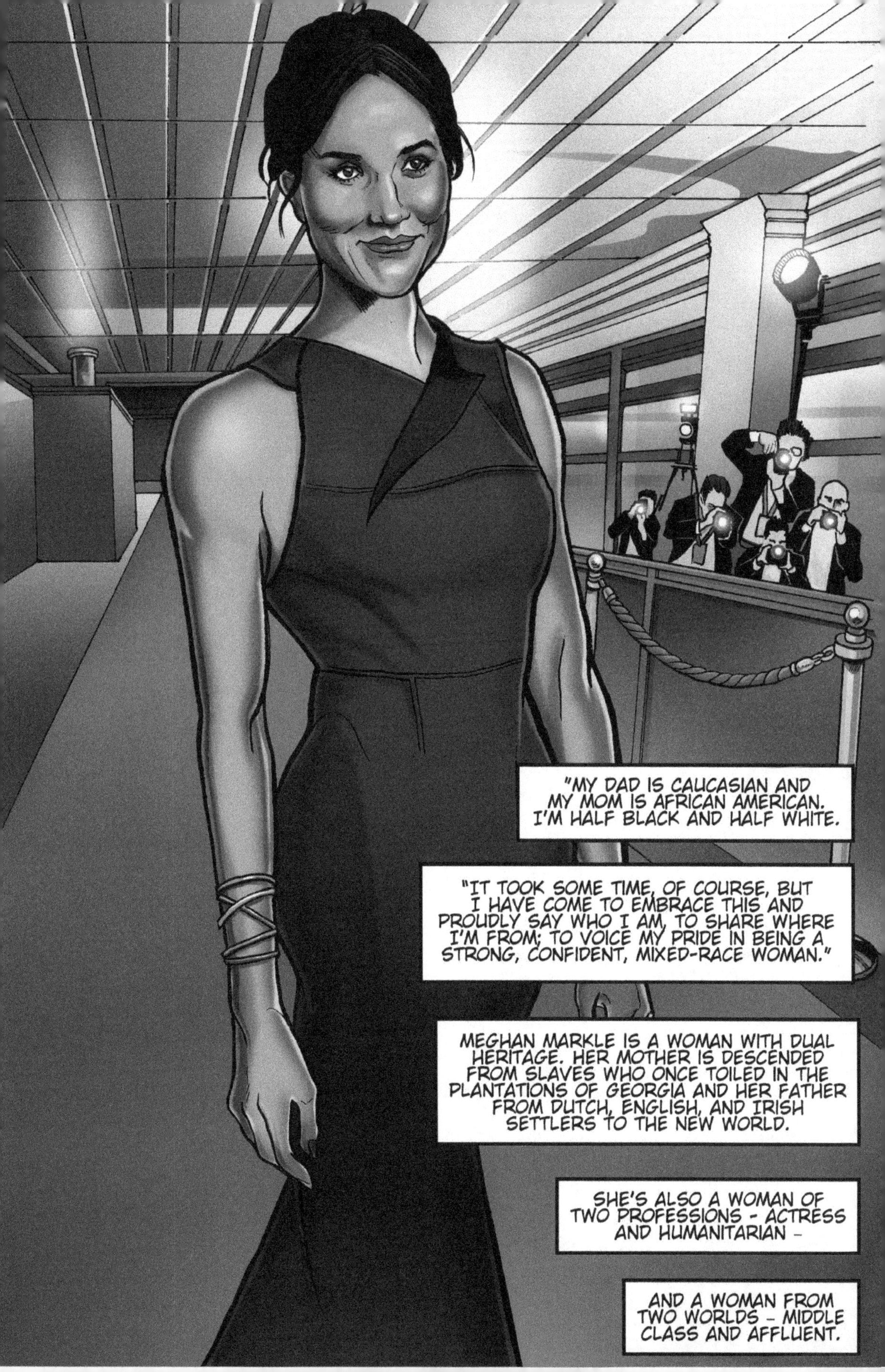
"MY DAD IS CAUCASIAN AND MY MOM IS AFRICAN AMERICAN. I'M HALF BLACK AND HALF WHITE.
"IT TOOK SOME TIME, OF COURSE, BUT I HAVE COME TO EMBRACE THIS AND PROUDLY SAY WHO I AM, TO SHARE WHERE I'M FROM; TO VOICE MY PRIDE IN BEING A STRONG, CONFIDENT, MIXED-RACE WOMAN."
MEGHAN MARKLE IS A WOMAN WITH DUAL HERITAGE. HER MOTHER IS DESCENDED FROM SLAVES WHO ONCE TOILED IN THE PLANTATIONS OF GEORGIA AND HER FATHER FROM DUTCH, ENGLISH, AND IRISH SETTLERS TO THE NEW WORLD.
SHE'S ALSO A WOMAN OF TWO PROFESSIONS - ACTRESS AND HUMANITARIAN -
AND A WOMAN FROM TWO WORLDS - MIDDLE CLASS AND AFFLUENT.

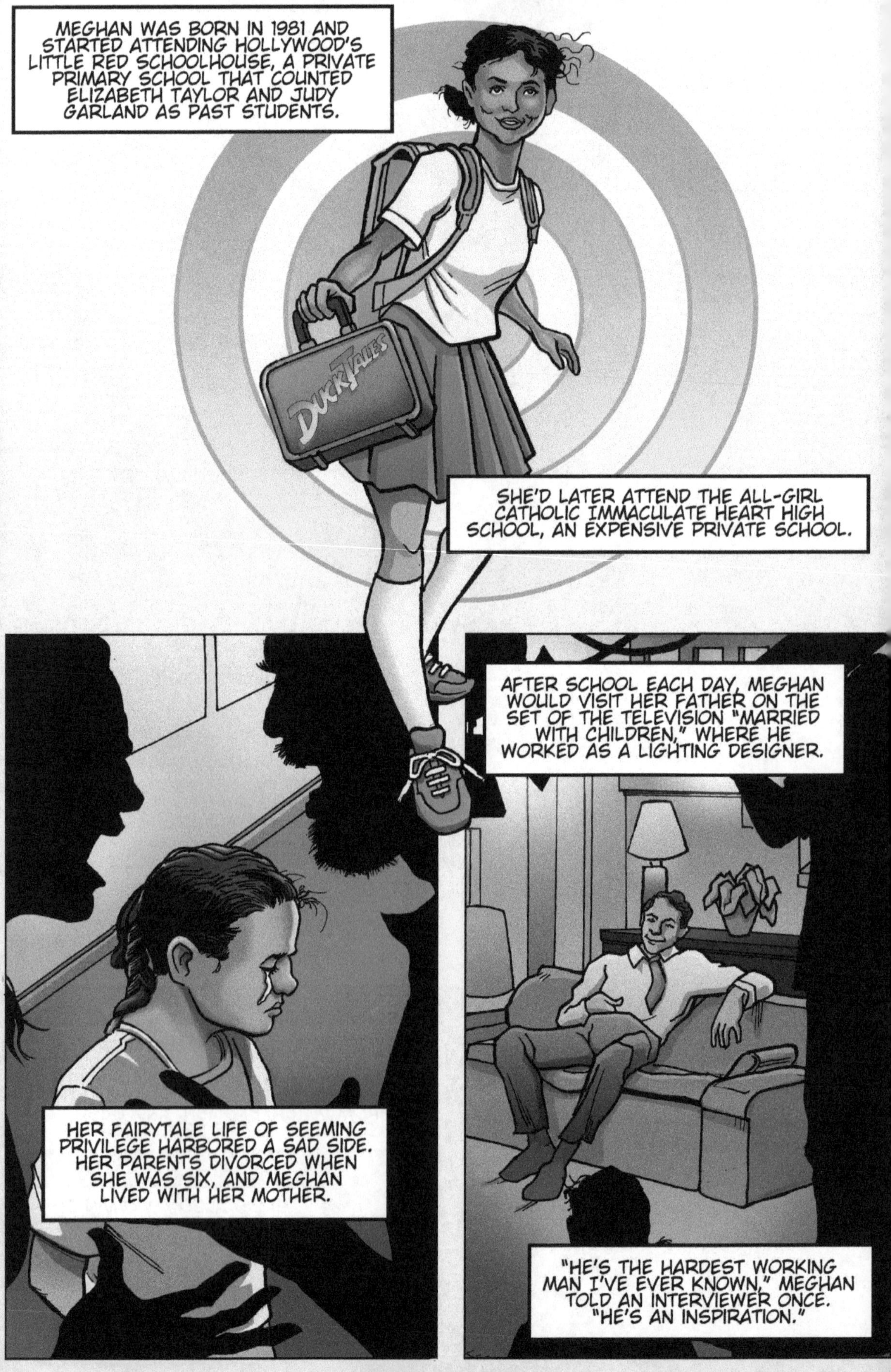
MEGHAN WAS BORN IN 1981 AND STARTED ATTENDING HOLLYWOOD'S LITTLE RED SCHOOLHOUSE, A PRIVATE PRIMARY SCHOOL THAT COUNTED ELIZABETH TAYLOR AND JUDY GARLAND AS PAST STUDENTS.
DUCKTALES
SHE'D LATER ATTEND THE ALL-GIRL CATHOLIC IMMACULATE HEART HIGH SCHOOL, AN EXPENSIVE PRIVATE SCHOOL.
HER FAIRYTALE LIFE OF SEEMING PRIVILEGE HARBORED A SAD SIDE. HER PARENTS DIVORCED WHEN SHE WAS SIX, AND MEGHAN LIVED WITH HER MOTHER.
AFTER SCHOOL EACH DAY, MEGHAN WOULD VISIT HER FATHER ON THE SET OF THE TELEVISION "MARRIED WITH CHILDREN," WHERE HE WORKED AS A LIGHTING DESIGNER.
"HE'S THE HARDEST WORKING MAN I'VE EVER KNOWN," MEGHAN TOLD AN INTERVIEWER ONCE. "HE'S AN INSPIRATION."

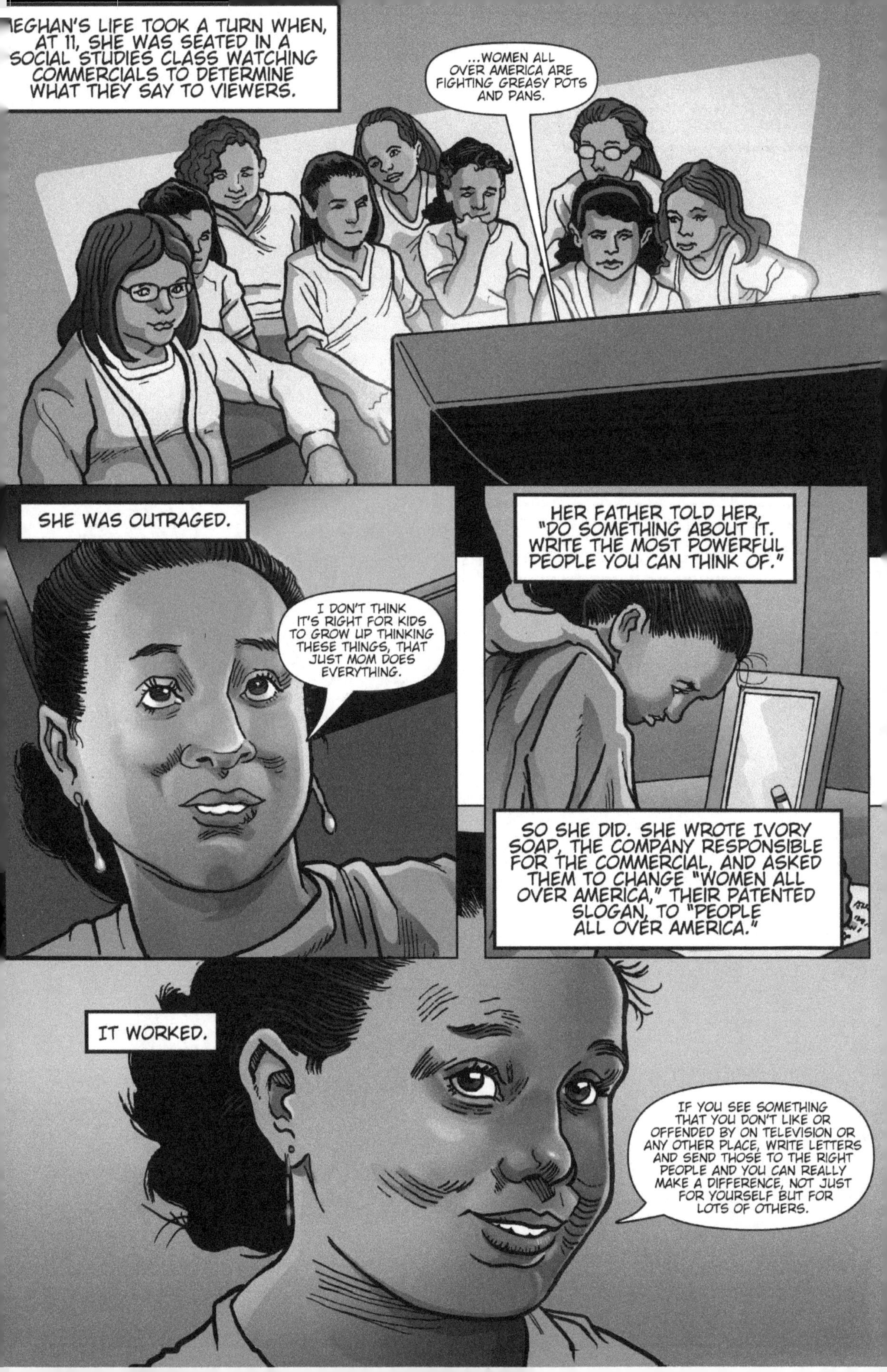

MEGHAN'S LIFE TOOK A TURN WHEN, AT 11, SHE WAS SEATED IN A SOCIAL STUDIES CLASS WATCHING COMMERCIALS TO DETERMINE WHAT THEY SAY TO VIEWERS.
...WOMEN ALL OVER AMERICA ARE FIGHTING GREASY POTS AND PANS.
SHE WAS OUTRAGED.
I DON'T THINK IT'S RIGHT FOR KIDS TO GROW UP THINKING THESE THINGS, THAT JUST MOM DOES EVERYTHING.
HER FATHER TOLD HER, "DO SOMETHING ABOUT IT. WRITE THE MOST POWERFUL PEOPLE YOU CAN THINK OF."
SO SHE DID. SHE WROTE IVORY SOAP, THE COMPANY RESPONSIBLE FOR THE COMMERCIAL, AND ASKED THEM TO CHANGE "WOMEN ALL OVER AMERICA," THEIR PATENTED SLOGAN, TO "PEOPLE ALL OVER AMERICA."
IT WORKED.
IF YOU SEE SOMETHING THAT YOU DON'T LIKE OR OFFENDED BY ON TELEVISION OR ANY OTHER PLACE, WRITE LETTERS AND SEND THOSE TO THE RIGHT PEOPLE AND YOU CAN REALLY MAKE A DIFFERENCE, NOT JUST FOR YOURSELF BUT FOR LOTS OF OTHERS.

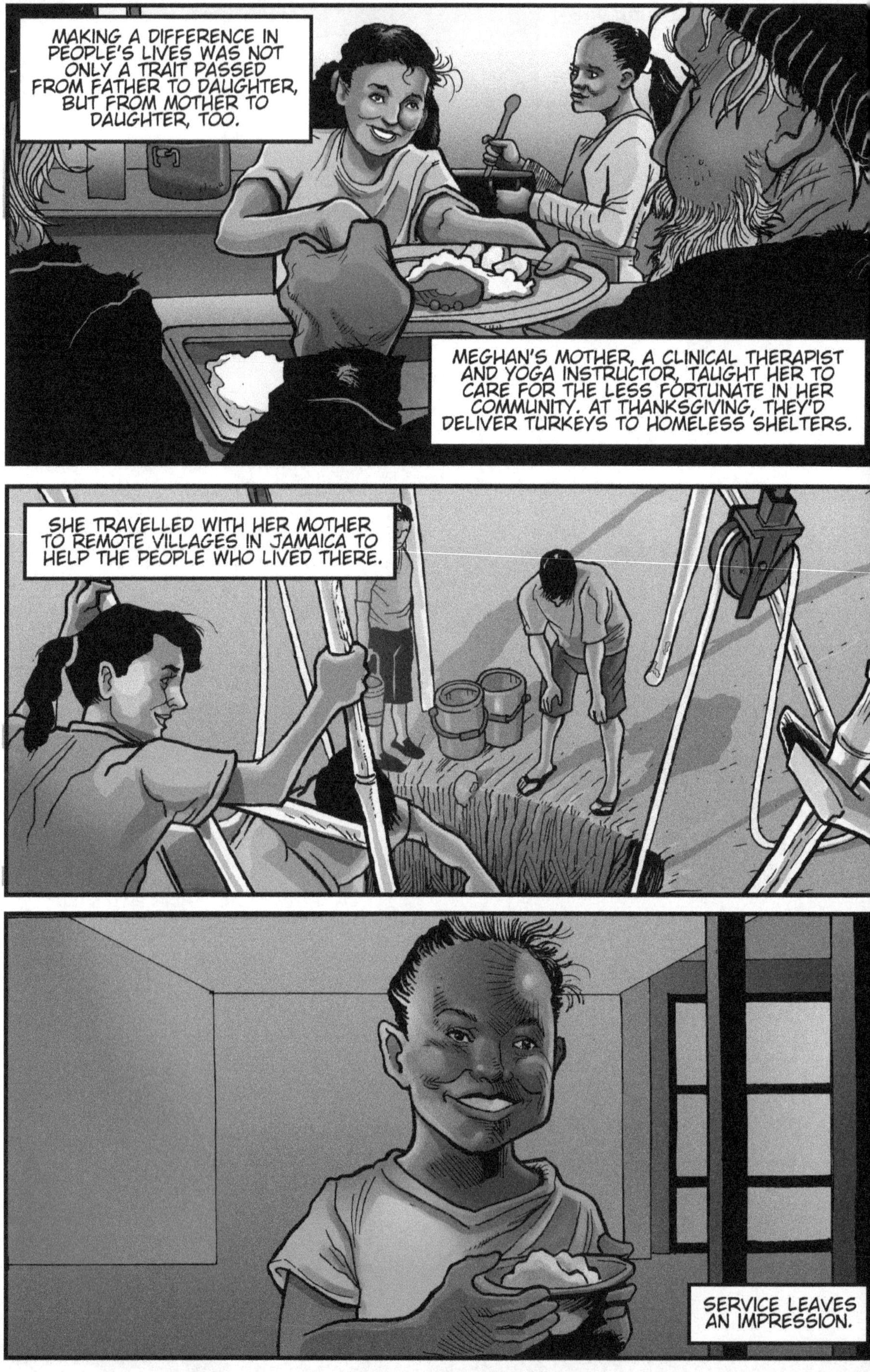
MAKING A DIFFERENCE IN PEOPLE'S LIVES WAS NOT ONLY A TRAIT PASSED FROM FATHER TO DAUGHTER, BUT FROM MOTHER TO DAUGHTER, TOO.
MEGHAN'S MOTHER, A CLINICAL THERAPIST AND YOGA INSTRUCTOR, TAUGHT HER TO CARE FOR THE LESS FORTUNATE IN HER COMMUNITY. AT THANKSGIVING, THEY'D DELIVER TURKEYS TO HOMELESS SHELTERS.
SHE TRAVELLED WITH HER MOTHER TO REMOTE VILLAGES IN JAMAICA TO HELP THE PEOPLE WHO LIVED THERE.
SERVICE LEAVES AN IMPRESSION.

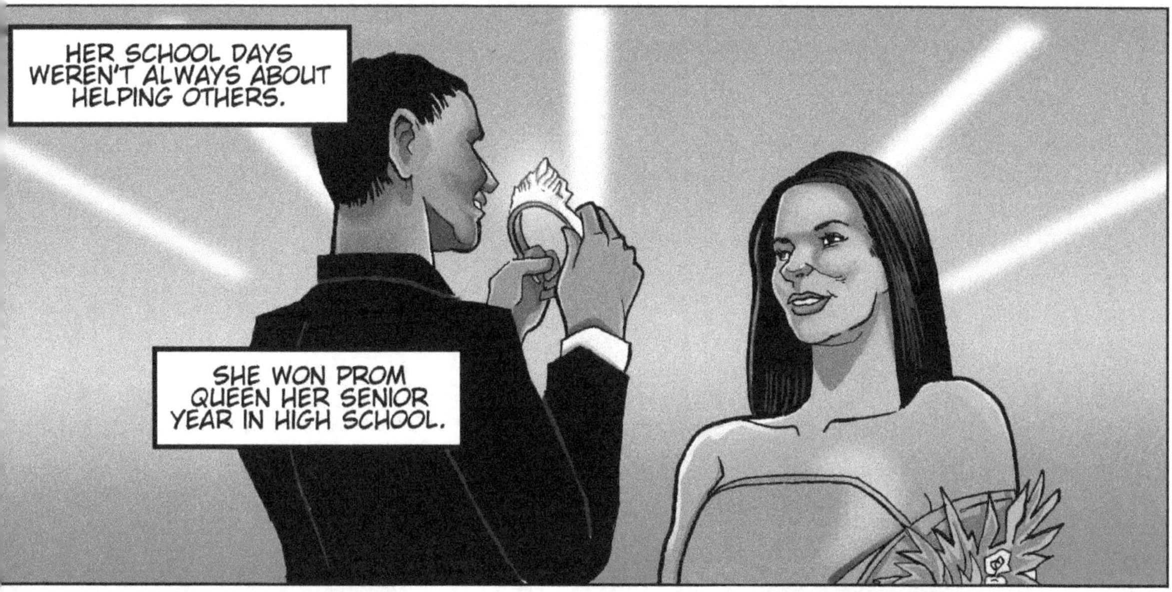
HER SCHOOL DAYS WEREN'T ALWAYS ABOUT HELPING OTHERS.
SHE WON PROM QUEEN HER SENIOR YEAR IN HIGH SCHOOL.

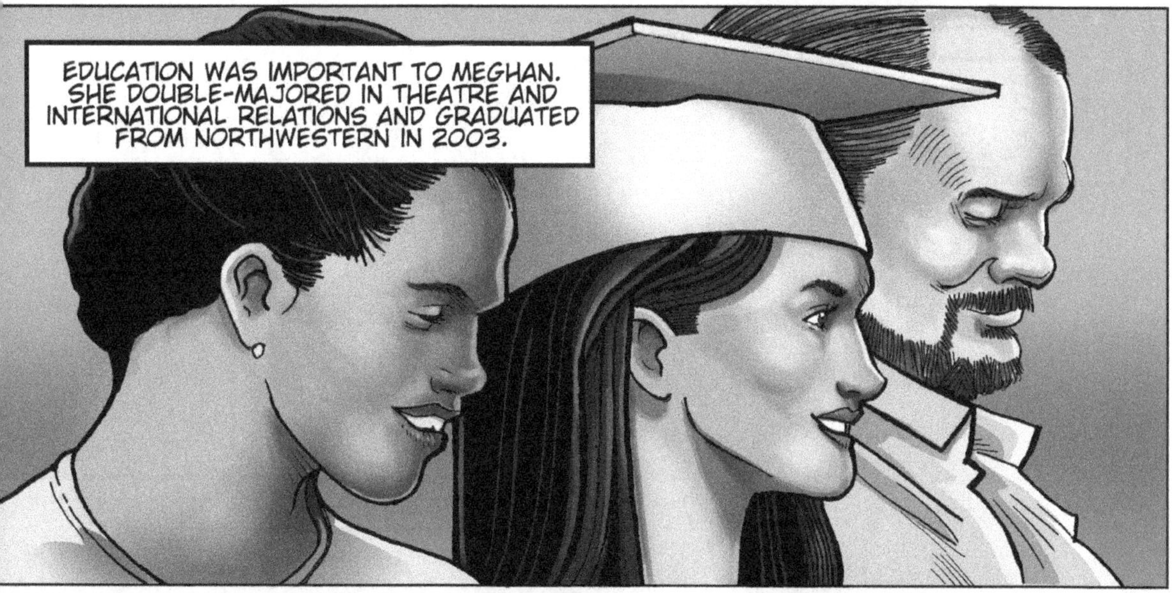
EDUCATION WAS IMPORTANT TO MEGHAN. SHE DOUBLE-MAJORED IN THEATRE AND INTERNATIONAL RELATIONS AND GRADUATED FROM NORTHWESTERN IN 2003.

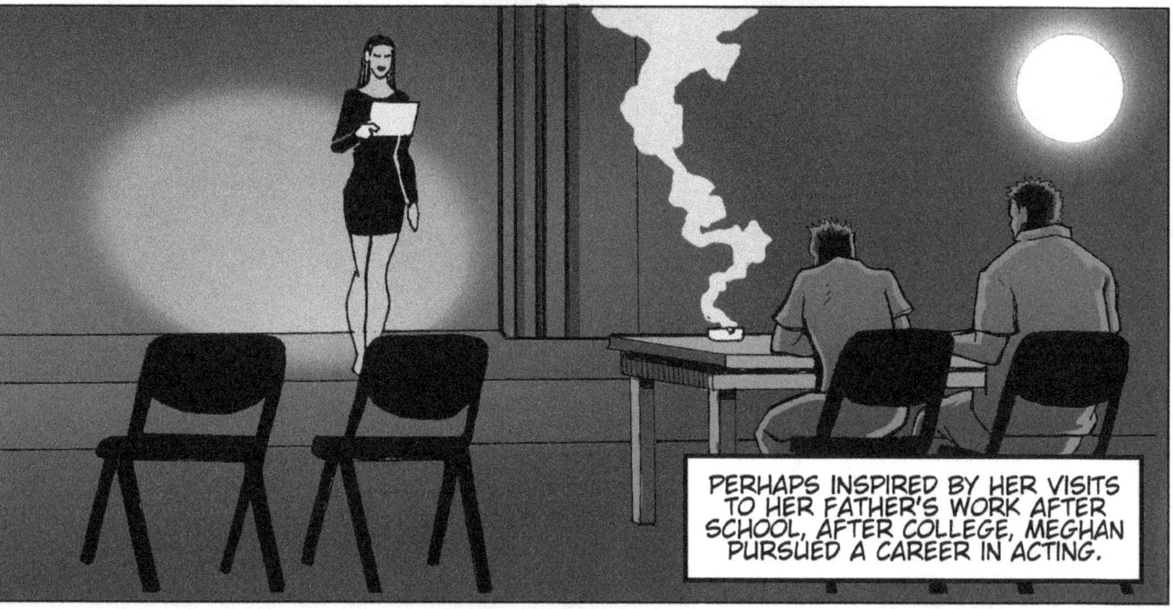
PERHAPS INSPIRED BY HER VISITS TO HER FATHER'S WORK AFTER SCHOOL, AFTER COLLEGE, MEGHAN PURSUED A CAREER IN ACTING.

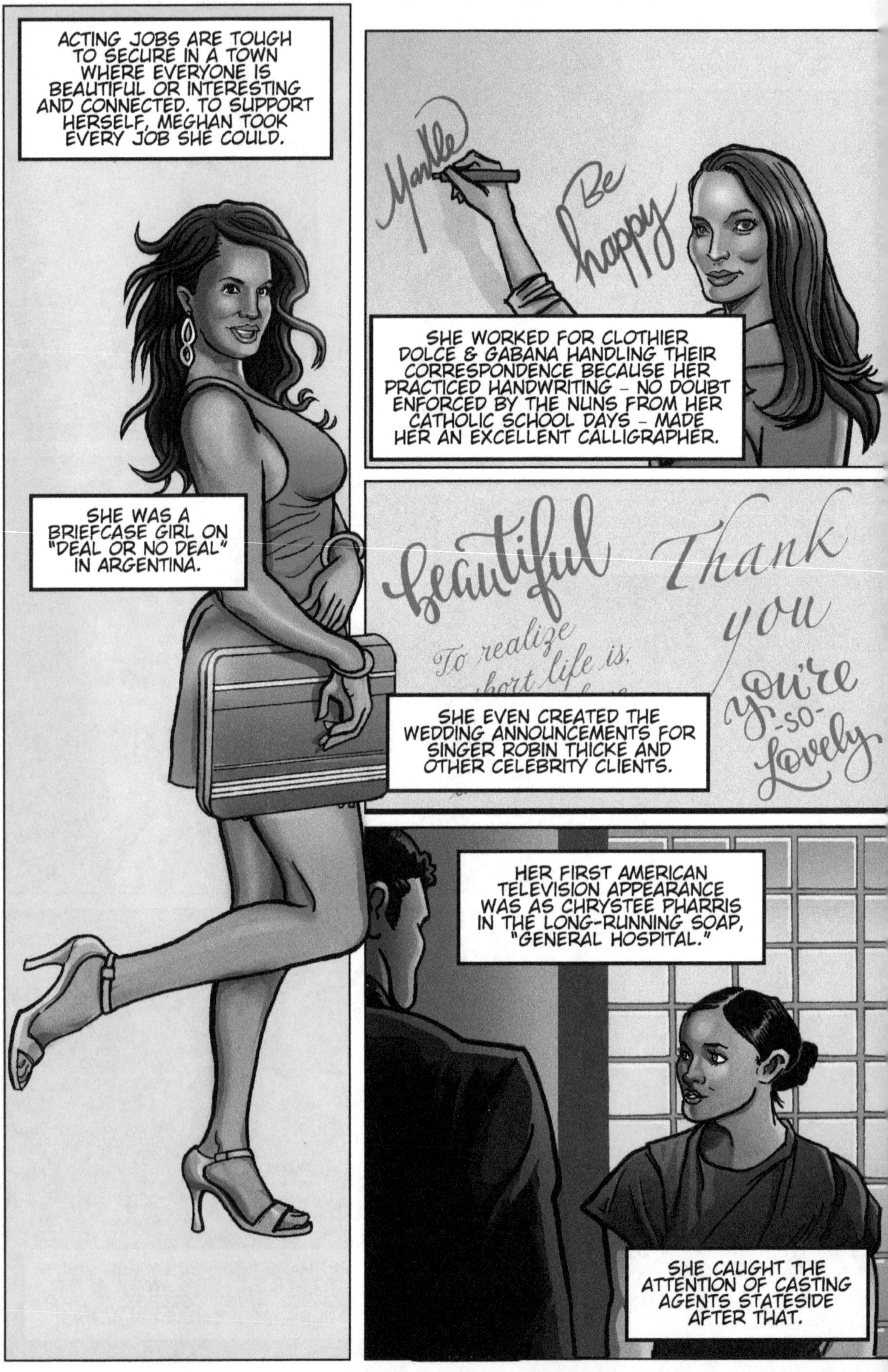
ACTING JOBS ARE TOUGH TO SECURE IN A TOWN WHERE EVERYONE IS BEAUTIFUL OR INTERESTING AND CONNECTED. TO SUPPORT HERSELF, MEGHAN TOOK EVERY JOB SHE COULD.
SHE WAS A BRIEFCASE GIRL ON "DEAL OR NO DEAL" IN ARGENTINA.
Be happy
SHE WORKED FOR CLOTHIER DOLCE & GABANA HANDLING THEIR CORRESPONDENCE BECAUSE HER PRACTICED HANDWRITING – NO DOUBT ENFORCED BY THE NUNS FROM HER CATHOLIC SCHOOL DAYS – MADE HER AN EXCELLENT CALLIGRAPHER.
beautiful
Thank you
To realize
you're -so- Lovely
SHE EVEN CREATED THE WEDDING ANNOUNCEMENTS FOR SINGER ROBIN THICKE AND OTHER CELEBRITY CLIENTS.
HER FIRST AMERICAN TELEVISION APPEARANCE WAS AS CHRYSTEE PHARRIS IN THE LONG-RUNNING SOAP, "GENERAL HOSPITAL."
SHE CAUGHT THE ATTENTION OF CASTING AGENTS STATESIDE AFTER THAT.

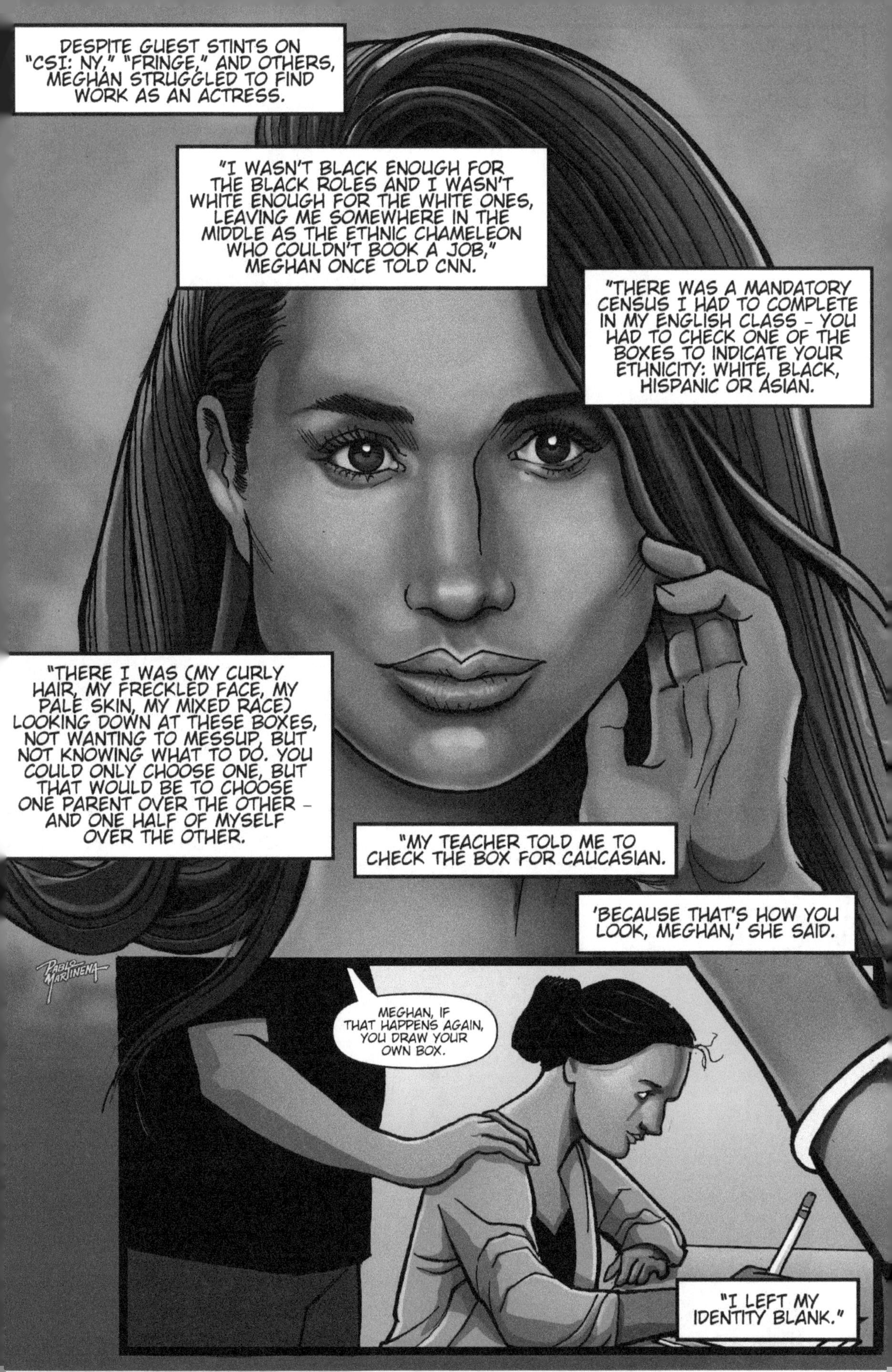
DESPITE GUEST STINTS ON "CSI: NY," "FRINGE," AND OTHERS, MEGHAN STRUGGLED TO FIND WORK AS AN ACTRESS.
"I WASN'T BLACK ENOUGH FOR THE BLACK ROLES AND I WASN'T WHITE ENOUGH FOR THE WHITE ONES, LEAVING ME SOMEWHERE IN THE MIDDLE AS THE ETHNIC CHAMELEON WHO COULDN'T BOOK A JOB," MEGHAN ONCE TOLD CNN.
"THERE WAS A MANDATORY CENSUS I HAD TO COMPLETE IN MY ENGLISH CLASS - YOU HAD TO CHECK ONE OF THE BOXES TO INDICATE YOUR ETHNICITY: WHITE, BLACK, HISPANIC OR ASIAN.
"THERE I WAS (MY CURLY HAIR, MY FRECKLED FACE, MY PALE SKIN, MY MIXED RACE) LOOKING DOWN AT THESE BOXES, NOT WANTING TO MESSUP, BUT NOT KNOWING WHAT TO DO. YOU COULD ONLY CHOOSE ONE, BUT THAT WOULD BE TO CHOOSE ONE PARENT OVER THE OTHER - AND ONE HALF OF MYSELF OVER THE OTHER.
"MY TEACHER TOLD ME TO CHECK THE BOX FOR CAUCASIAN.
'BECAUSE THAT'S HOW YOU LOOK, MEGHAN,' SHE SAID.
PABLO MARTINENA
MEGHAN, IF THAT HAPPENS AGAIN, YOU DRAW YOUR OWN BOX.
"I LEFT MY IDENTITY BLANK."

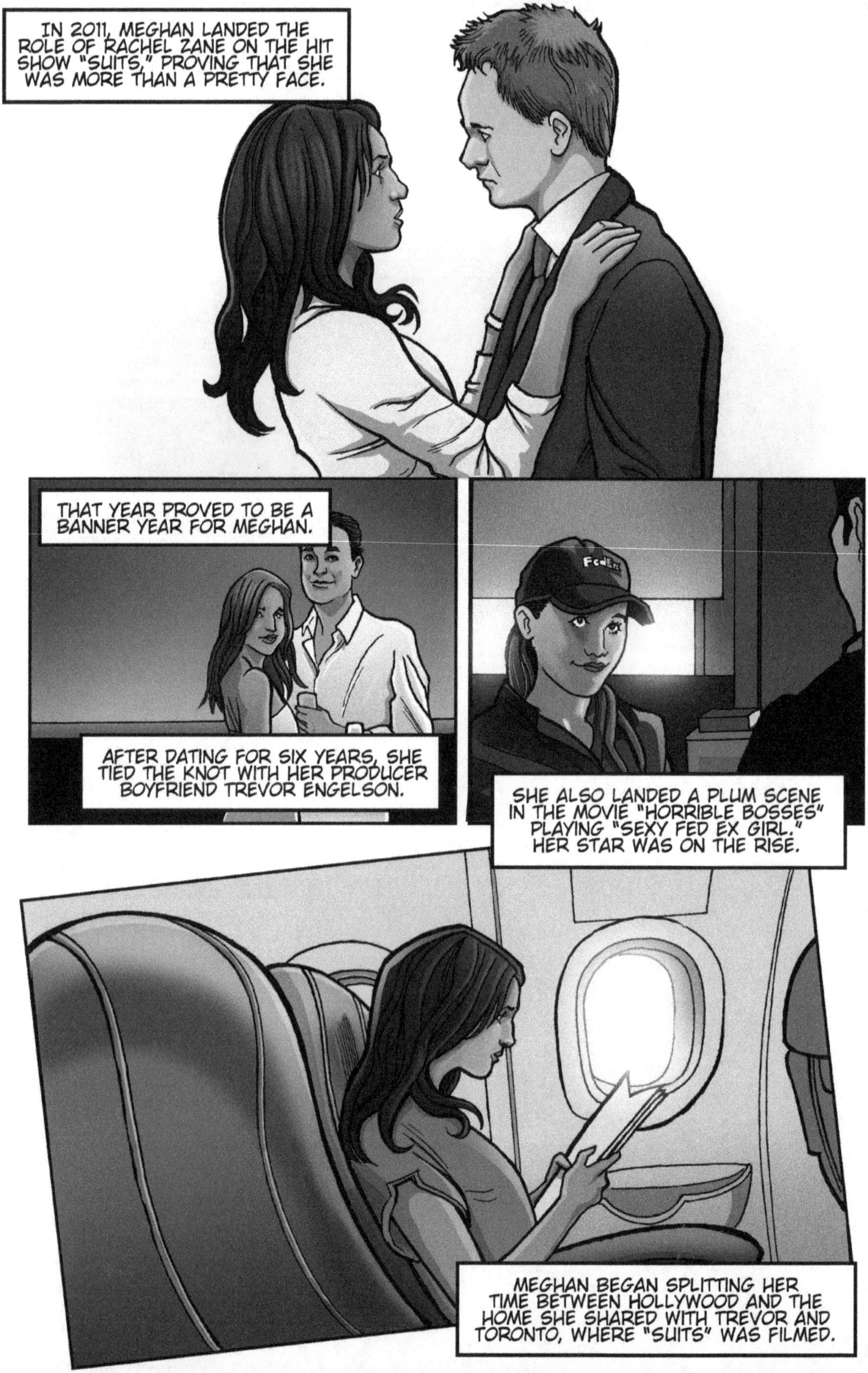
IN 2011, MEGHAN LANDED THE ROLE OF RACHEL ZANE ON THE HIT SHOW "SUITS," PROVING THAT SHE WAS MORE THAN A PRETTY FACE.
THAT YEAR PROVED TO BE A BANNER YEAR FOR MEGHAN.
AFTER DATING FOR SIX YEARS, SHE TIED THE KNOT WITH HER PRODUCER BOYFRIEND TREVOR ENGELSON.
SHE ALSO LANDED A PLUM SCENE IN THE MOVIE "HORRIBLE BOSSES" PLAYING "SEXY FED EX GIRL." HER STAR WAS ON THE RISE.
MEGHAN BEGAN SPLITTING HER TIME BETWEEN HOLLYWOOD AND THE HOME SHE SHARED WITH TREVOR AND TORONTO, WHERE "SUITS" WAS FILMED.

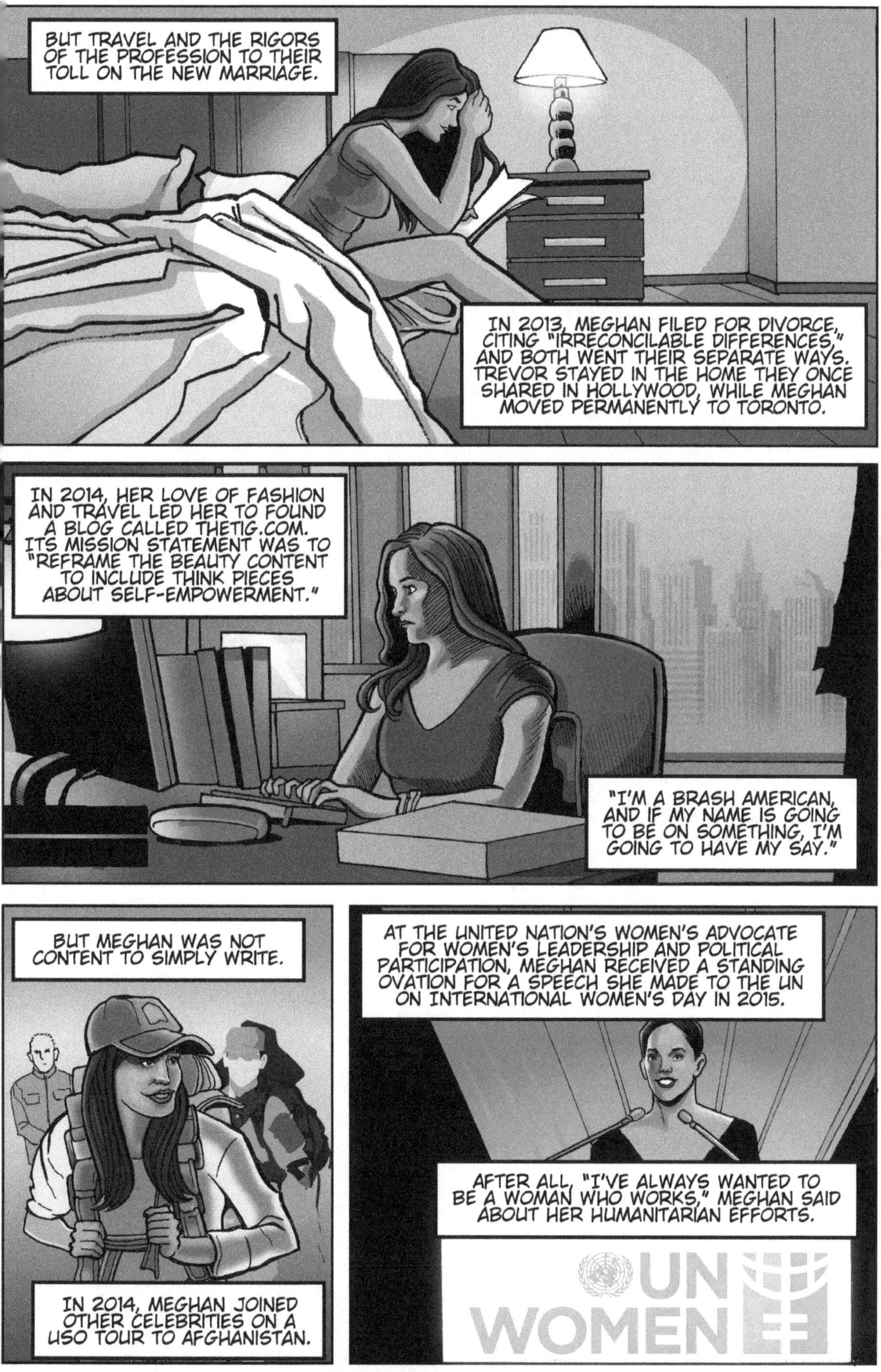
BUT TRAVEL AND THE RIGORS OF THE PROFESSION TO THEIR TOLL ON THE NEW MARRIAGE.
IN 2013, MEGHAN FILED FOR DIVORCE, CITING "IRRECONCILABLE DIFFERENCES," AND BOTH WENT THEIR SEPARATE WAYS. TREVOR STAYED IN THE HOME THEY ONCE SHARED IN HOLLYWOOD, WHILE MEGHAN MOVED PERMANENTLY TO TORONTO.
IN 2014, HER LOVE OF FASHION AND TRAVEL LED HER TO FOUND A BLOG CALLED THETIG.COM. ITS MISSION STATEMENT WAS TO "REFRAME THE BEAUTY CONTENT TO INCLUDE THINK PIECES ABOUT SELF-EMPOWERMENT."
"I'M A BRASH AMERICAN, AND IF MY NAME IS GOING TO BE ON SOMETHING, I'M GOING TO HAVE MY SAY."
BUT MEGHAN WAS NOT CONTENT TO SIMPLY WRITE.
IN 2014, MEGHAN JOINED OTHER CELEBRITIES ON A USO TOUR TO AFGHANISTAN.
AT THE UNITED NATION'S WOMEN'S ADVOCATE FOR WOMEN'S LEADERSHIP AND POLITICAL PARTICIPATION, MEGHAN RECEIVED A STANDING OVATION FOR A SPEECH SHE MADE TO THE UN ON INTERNATIONAL WOMEN'S DAY IN 2015.
AFTER ALL, "I'VE ALWAYS WANTED TO BE A WOMAN WHO WORKS," MEGHAN SAID ABOUT HER HUMANITARIAN EFFORTS.
UN WOMEN

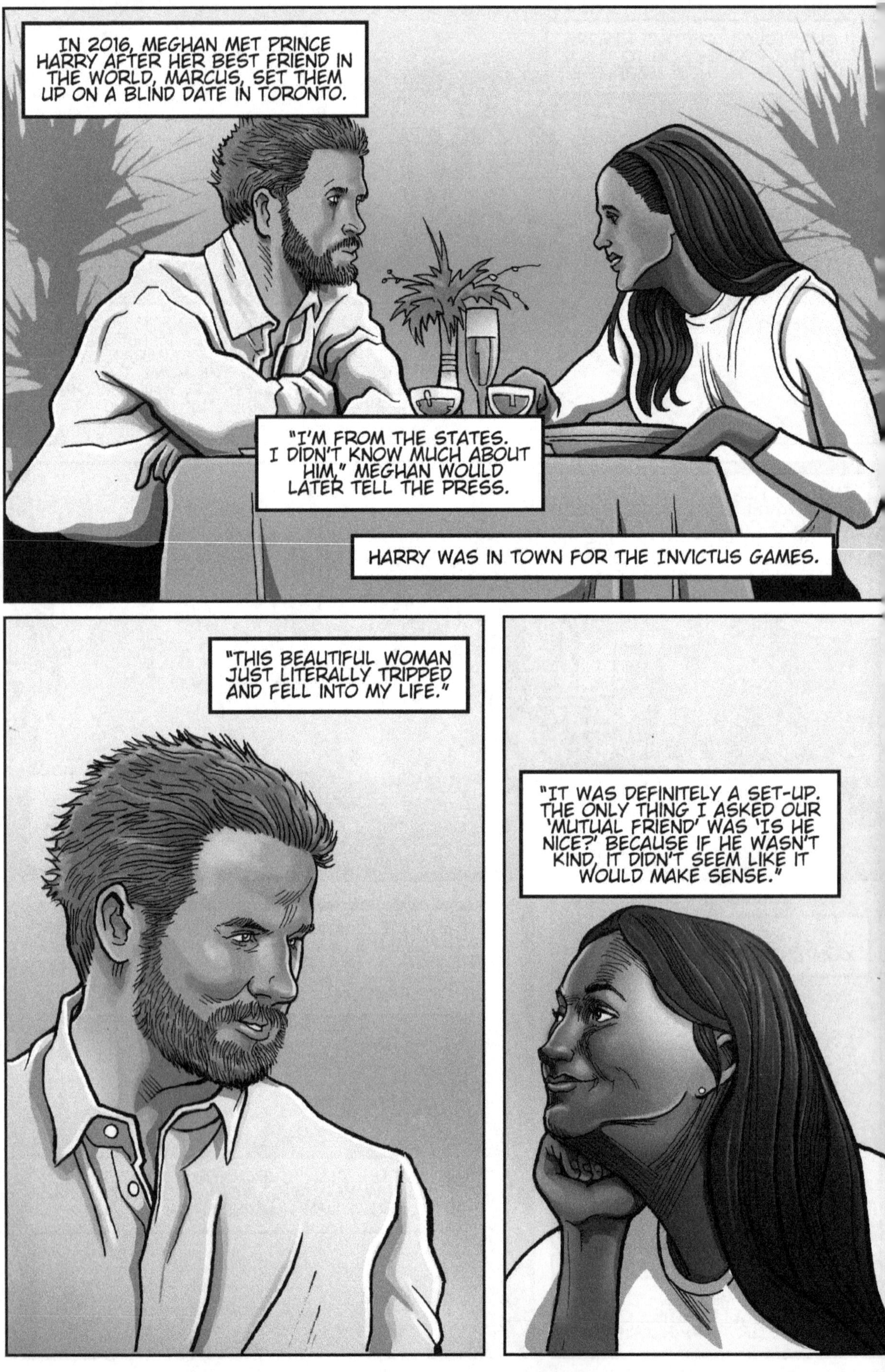
IN 2016, MEGHAN MET PRINCE HARRY AFTER HER BEST FRIEND IN THE WORLD, MARCUS, SET THEM UP ON A BLIND DATE IN TORONTO.
"I'M FROM THE STATES. I DIDN'T KNOW MUCH ABOUT HIM," MEGHAN WOULD LATER TELL THE PRESS.
HARRY WAS IN TOWN FOR THE INVICTUS GAMES.
"THIS BEAUTIFUL WOMAN JUST LITERALLY TRIPPED AND FELL INTO MY LIFE."
"IT WAS DEFINITELY A SET-UP. THE ONLY THING I ASKED OUR 'MUTUAL FRIEND' WAS 'IS HE NICE?' BECAUSE IF HE WASN'T KIND, IT DIDN'T SEEM LIKE IT WOULD MAKE SENSE."

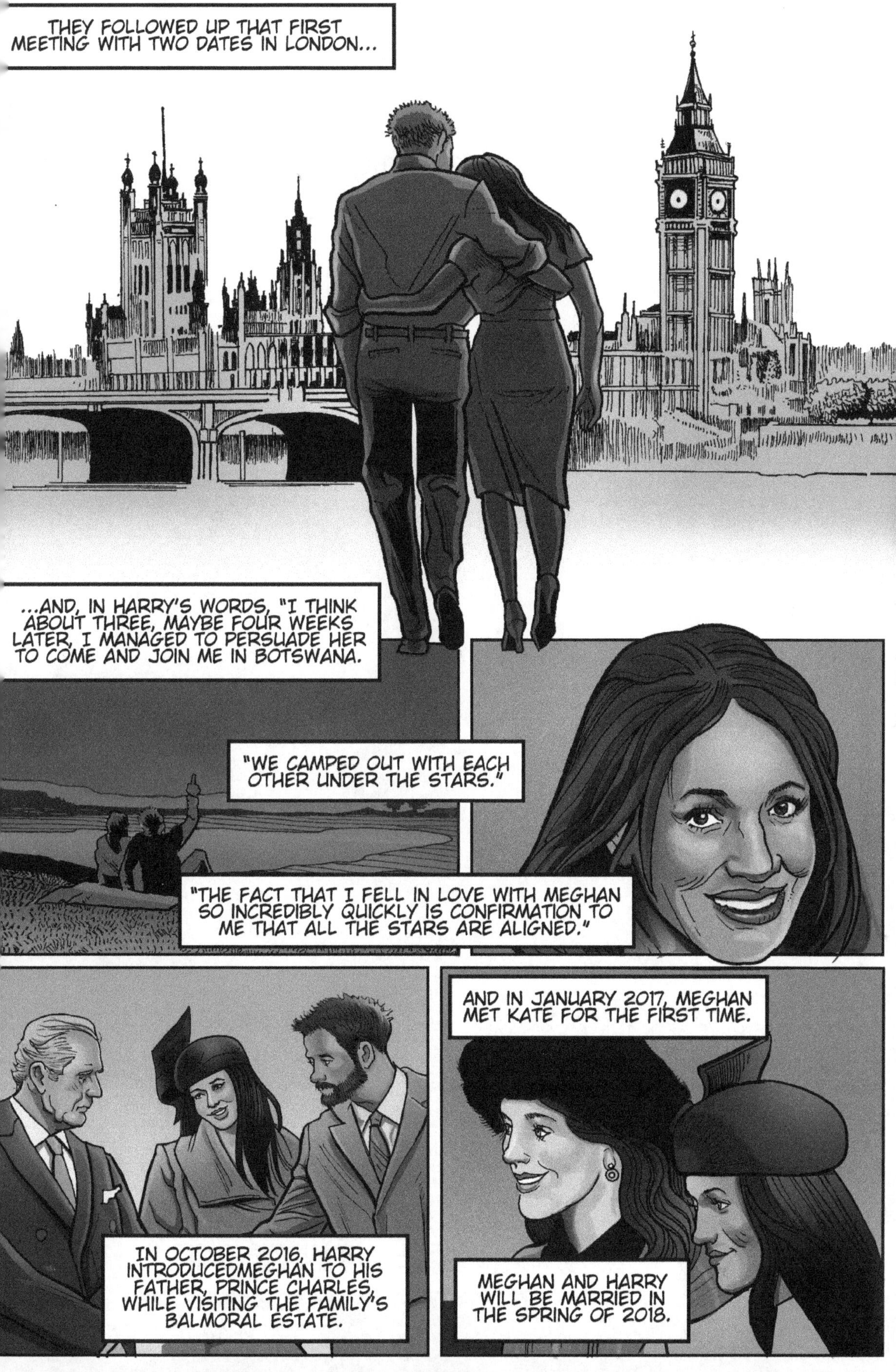
THEY FOLLOWED UP THAT FIRST MEETING WITH TWO DATES IN LONDON...
...AND, IN HARRY'S WORDS, "I THINK ABOUT THREE, MAYBE FOUR WEEKS LATER, I MANAGED TO PERSUADE HER TO COME AND JOIN ME IN BOTSWANA.
"WE CAMPED OUT WITH EACH OTHER UNDER THE STARS."
"THE FACT THAT I FELL IN LOVE WITH MEGHAN SO INCREDIBLY QUICKLY IS CONFIRMATION TO ME THAT ALL THE STARS ARE ALIGNED."
IN OCTOBER 2016, HARRY INTRODUCEDMEGHAN TO HIS FATHER, PRINCE CHARLES, WHILE VISITING THE FAMILY'S BALMORAL ESTATE.
AND IN JANUARY 2017, MEGHAN MET KATE FOR THE FIRST TIME.
MEGHAN AND HARRY WILL BE MARRIED IN THE SPRING OF 2018.

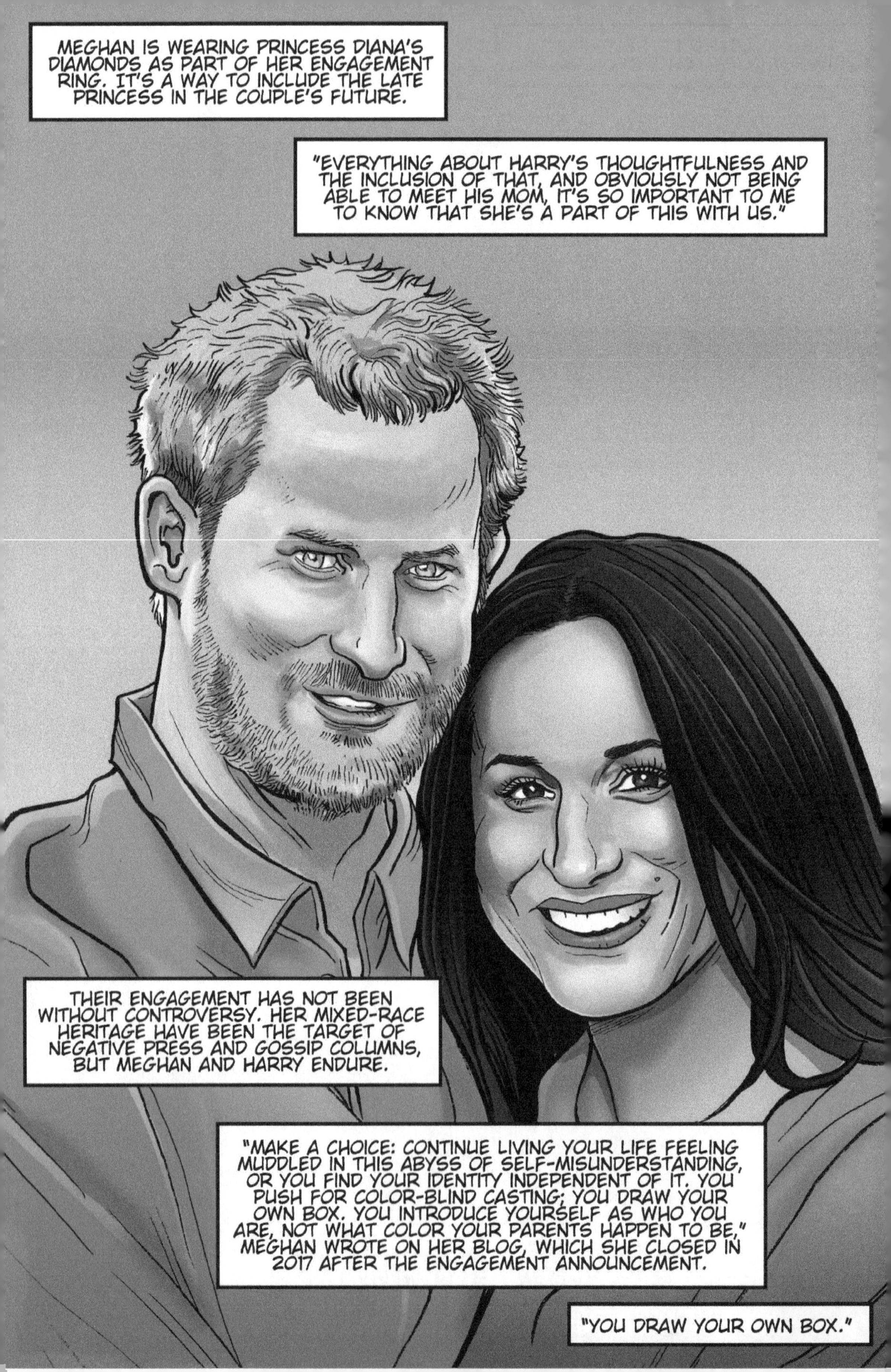
MEGHAN IS WEARING PRINCESS DIANA'S DIAMONDS AS PART OF HER ENGAGEMENT RING. IT'S A WAY TO INCLUDE THE LATE PRINCESS IN THE COUPLE'S FUTURE.
"EVERYTHING ABOUT HARRY'S THOUGHTFULNESS AND THE INCLUSION OF THAT, AND OBVIOUSLY NOT BEING ABLE TO MEET HIS MOM, IT'S SO IMPORTANT TO ME TO KNOW THAT SHE'S A PART OF THIS WITH US."
THEIR ENGAGEMENT HAS NOT BEEN WITHOUT CONTROVERSY. HER MIXED-RACE HERITAGE HAVE BEEN THE TARGET OF NEGATIVE PRESS AND GOSSIP COLUMNS, BUT MEGHAN AND HARRY ENDURE.
"MAKE A CHOICE: CONTINUE LIVING YOUR LIFE FEELING MUDDLED IN THIS ABYSS OF SELF-MISUNDERSTANDING, OR YOU FIND YOUR IDENTITY INDEPENDENT OF IT. YOU PUSH FOR COLOR-BLIND CASTING; YOU DRAW YOUR OWN BOX. YOU INTRODUCE YOURSELF AS WHO YOU ARE, NOT WHAT COLOR YOUR PARENTS HAPPEN TO BE," MEGHAN WROTE ON HER BLOG, WHICH SHE CLOSED IN 2017 AFTER THE ENGAGEMENT ANNOUNCEMENT.
"YOU DRAW YOUR OWN BOX."

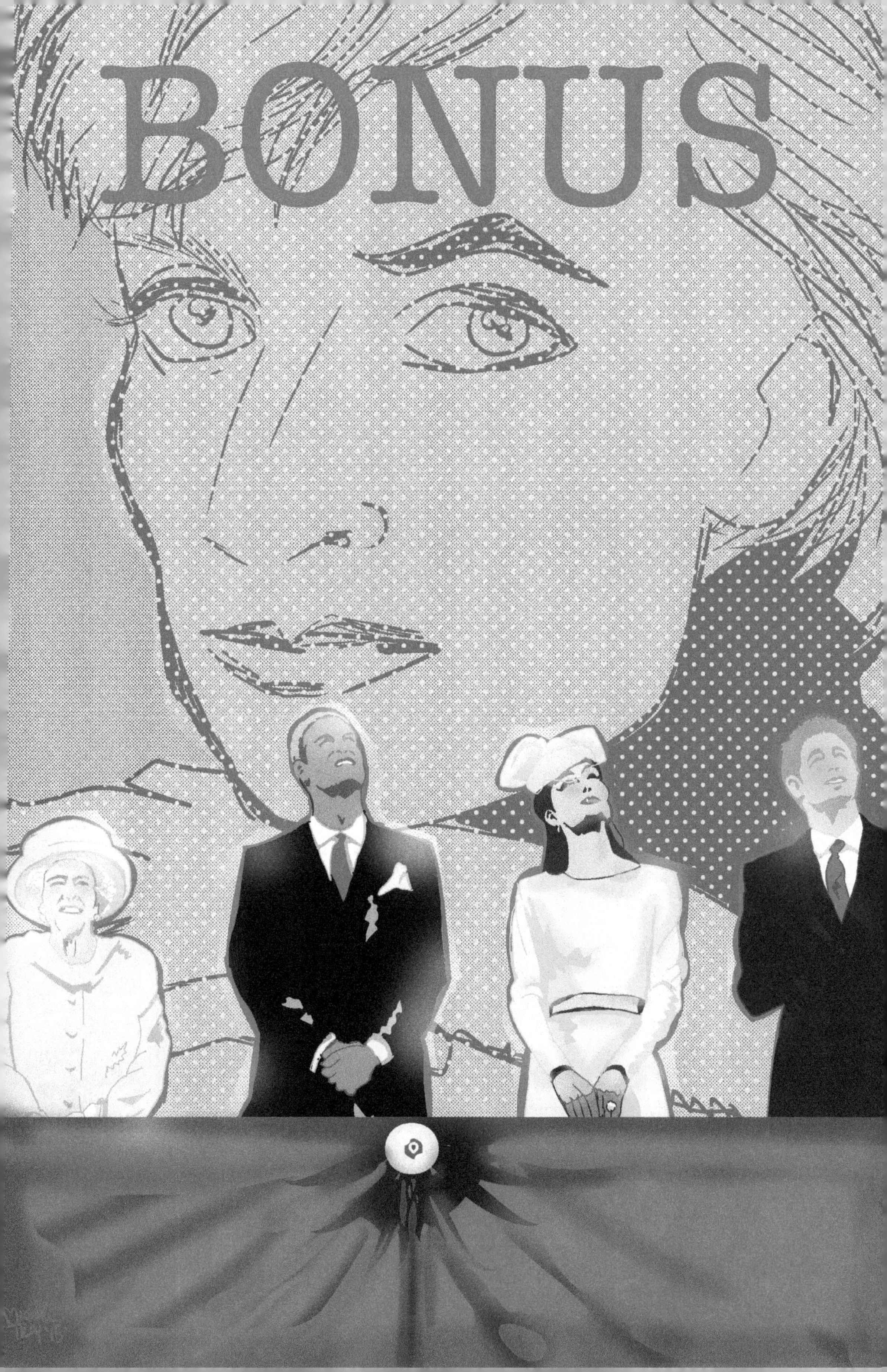
BONUS

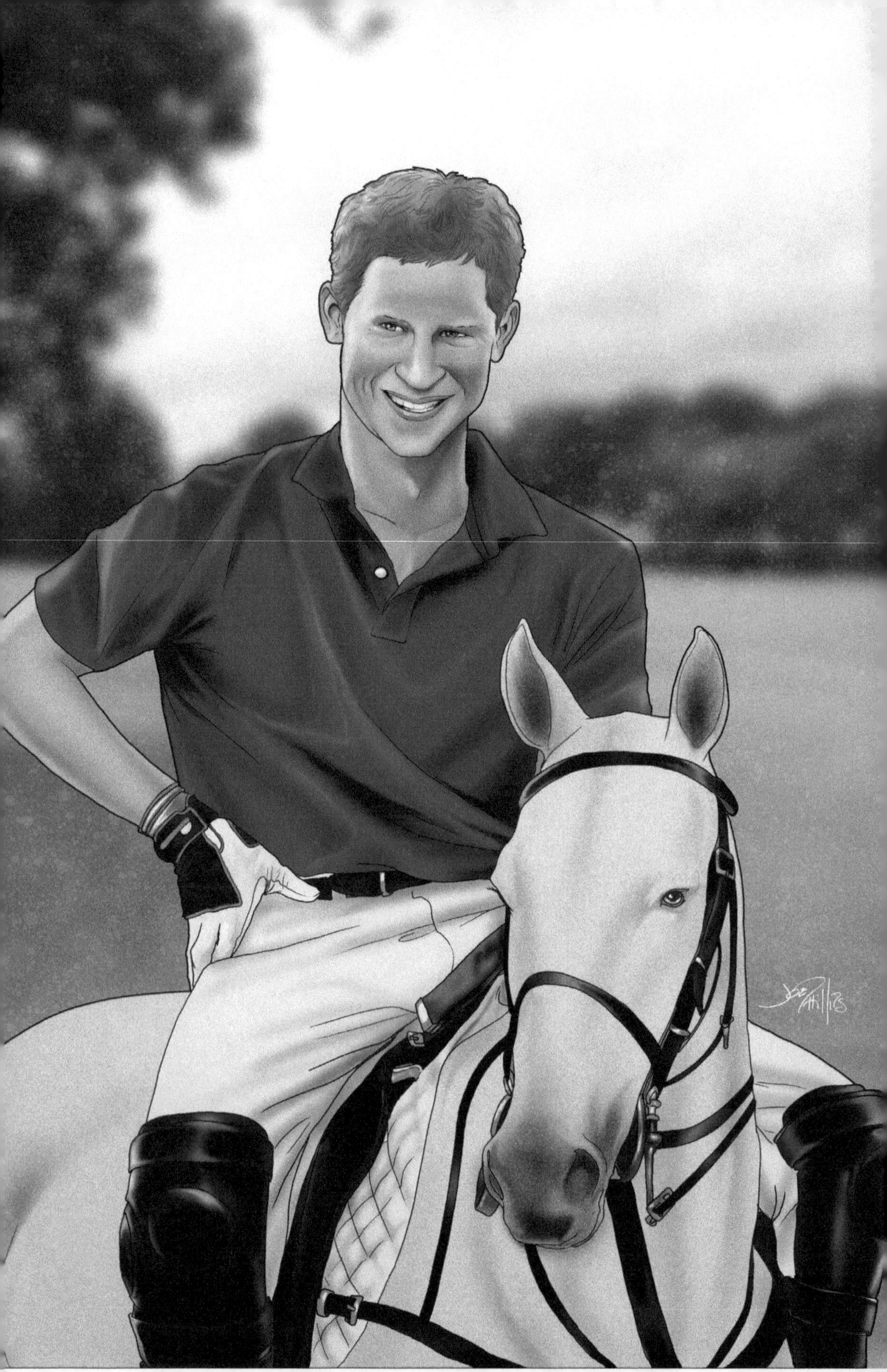

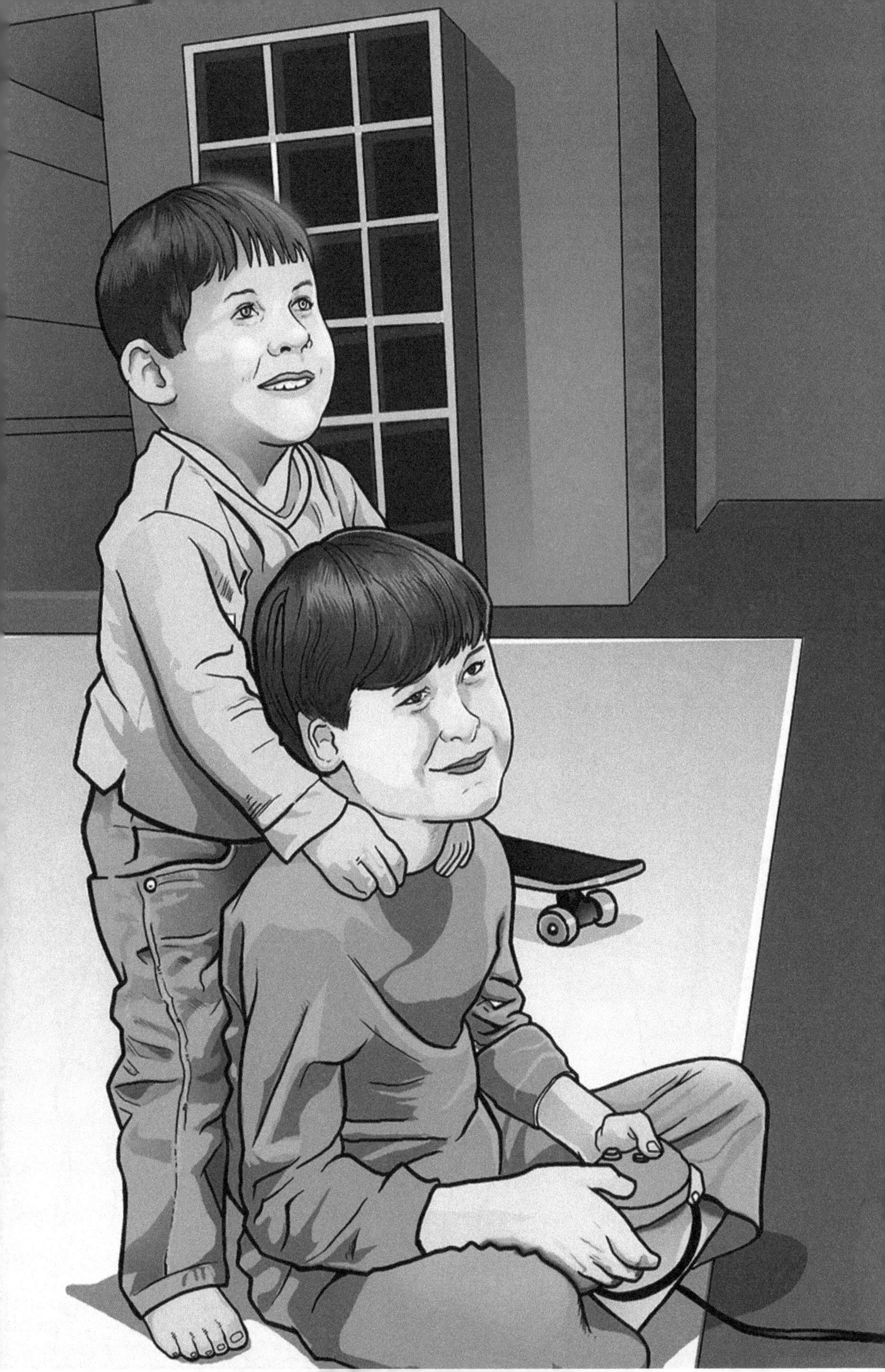

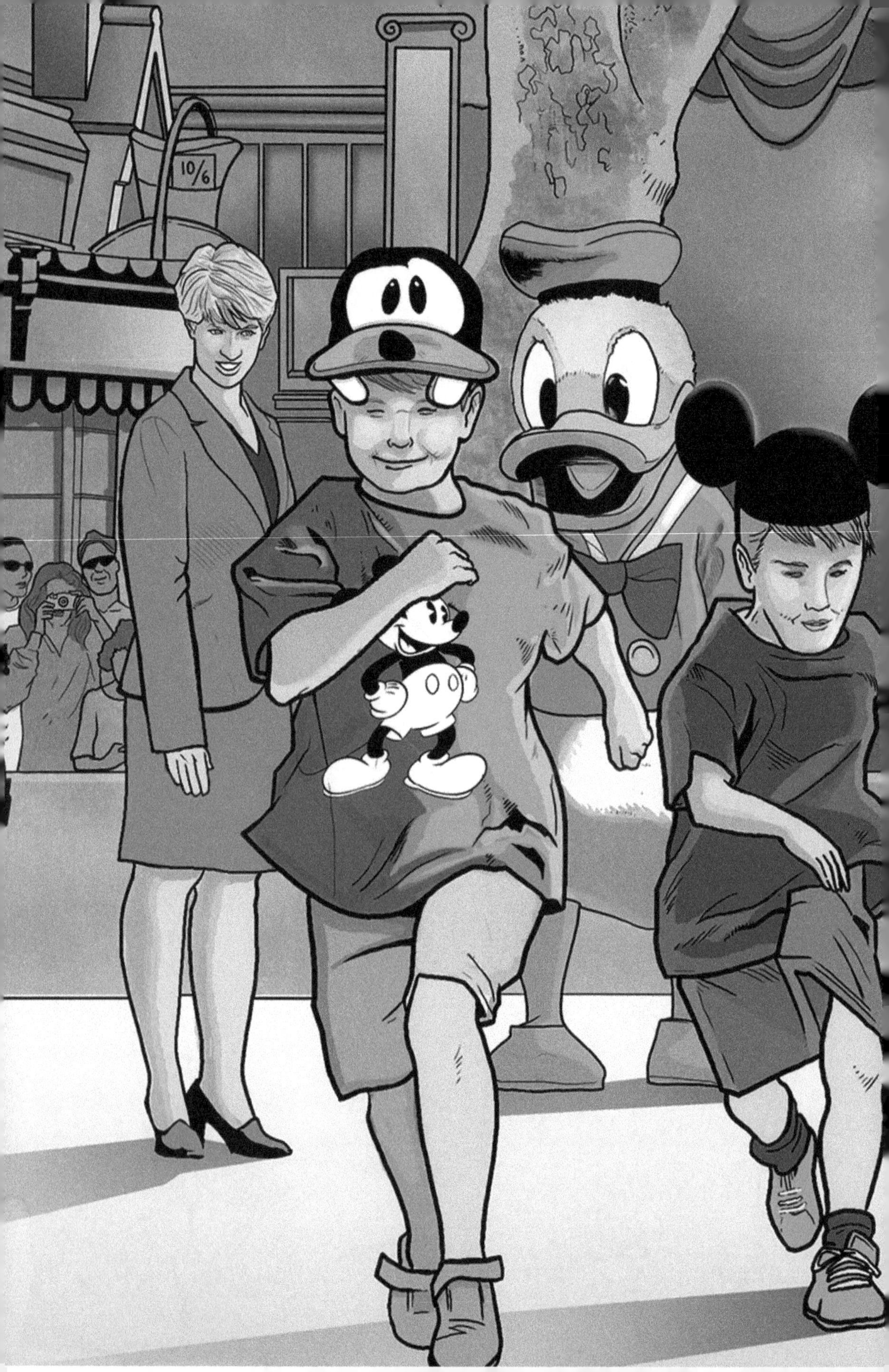
10/6

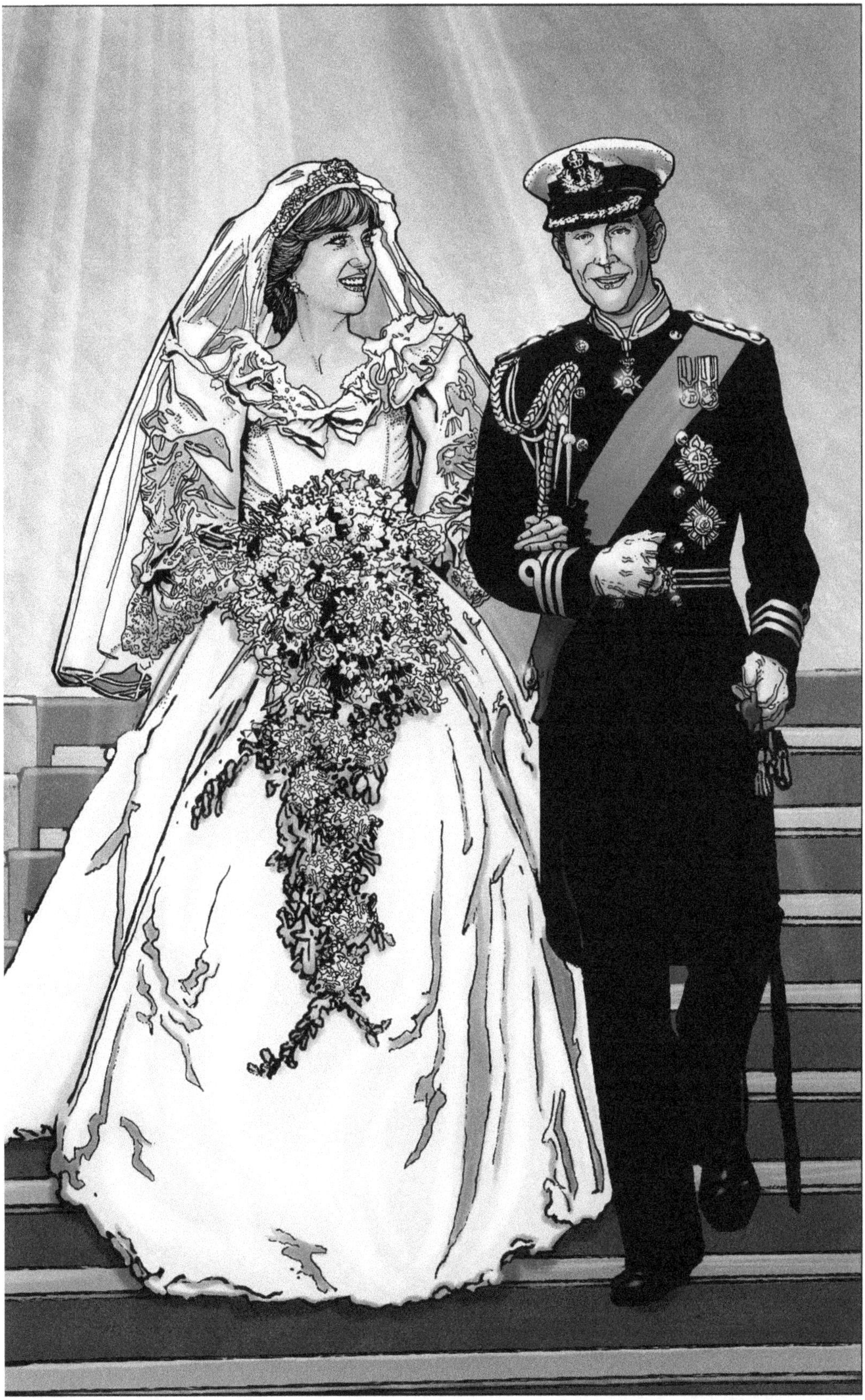

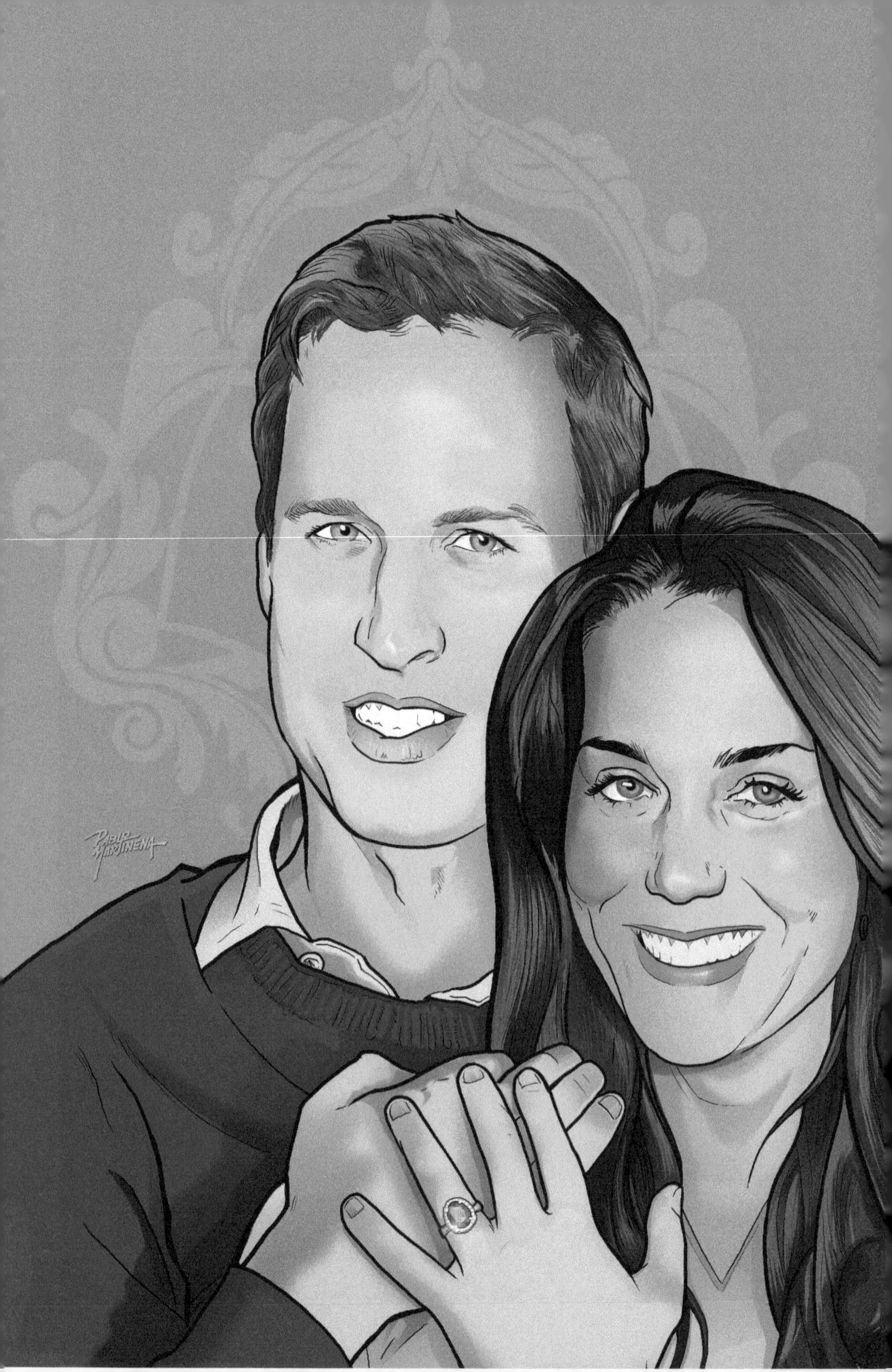
PABLO MARTINENA

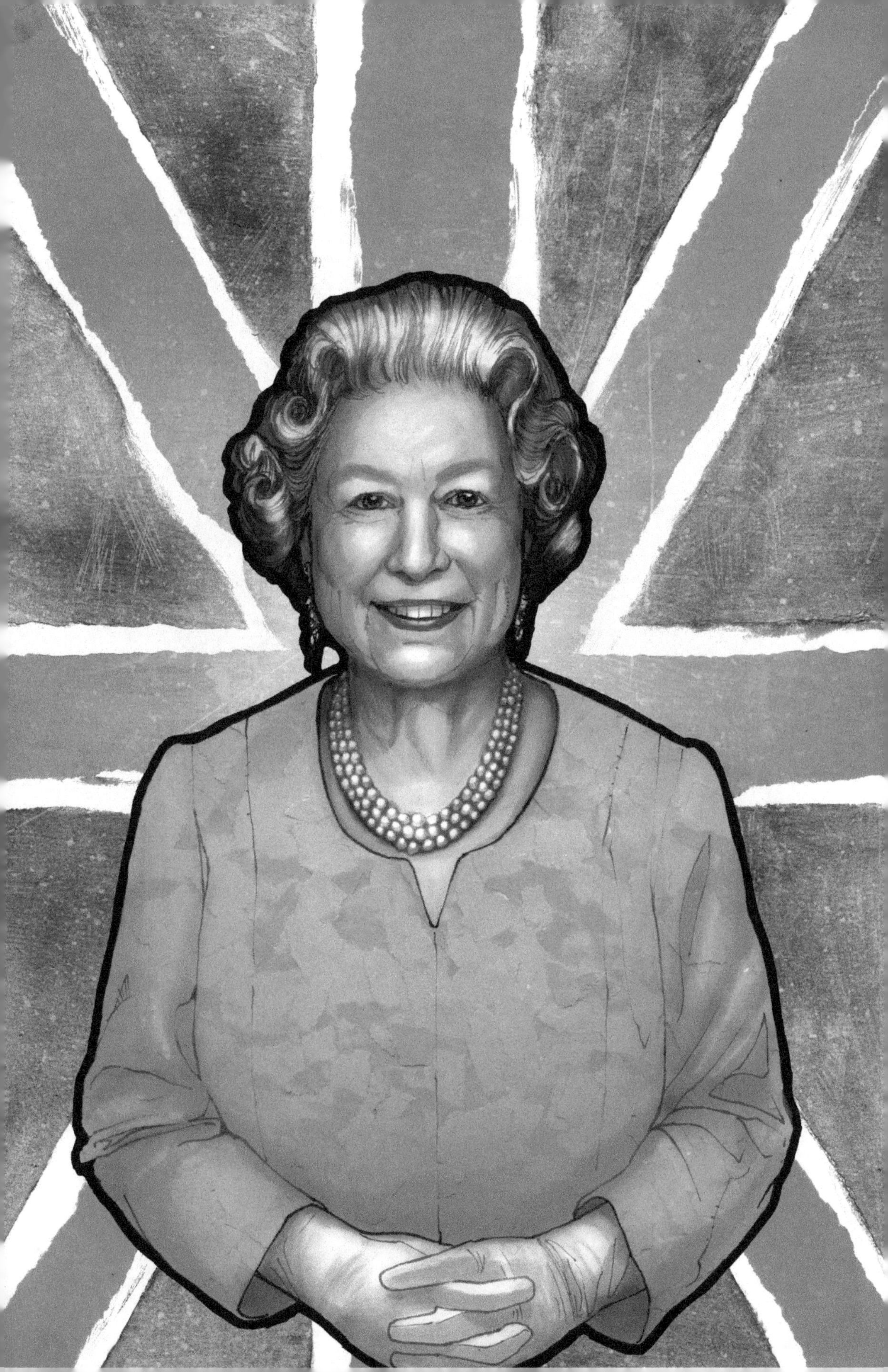

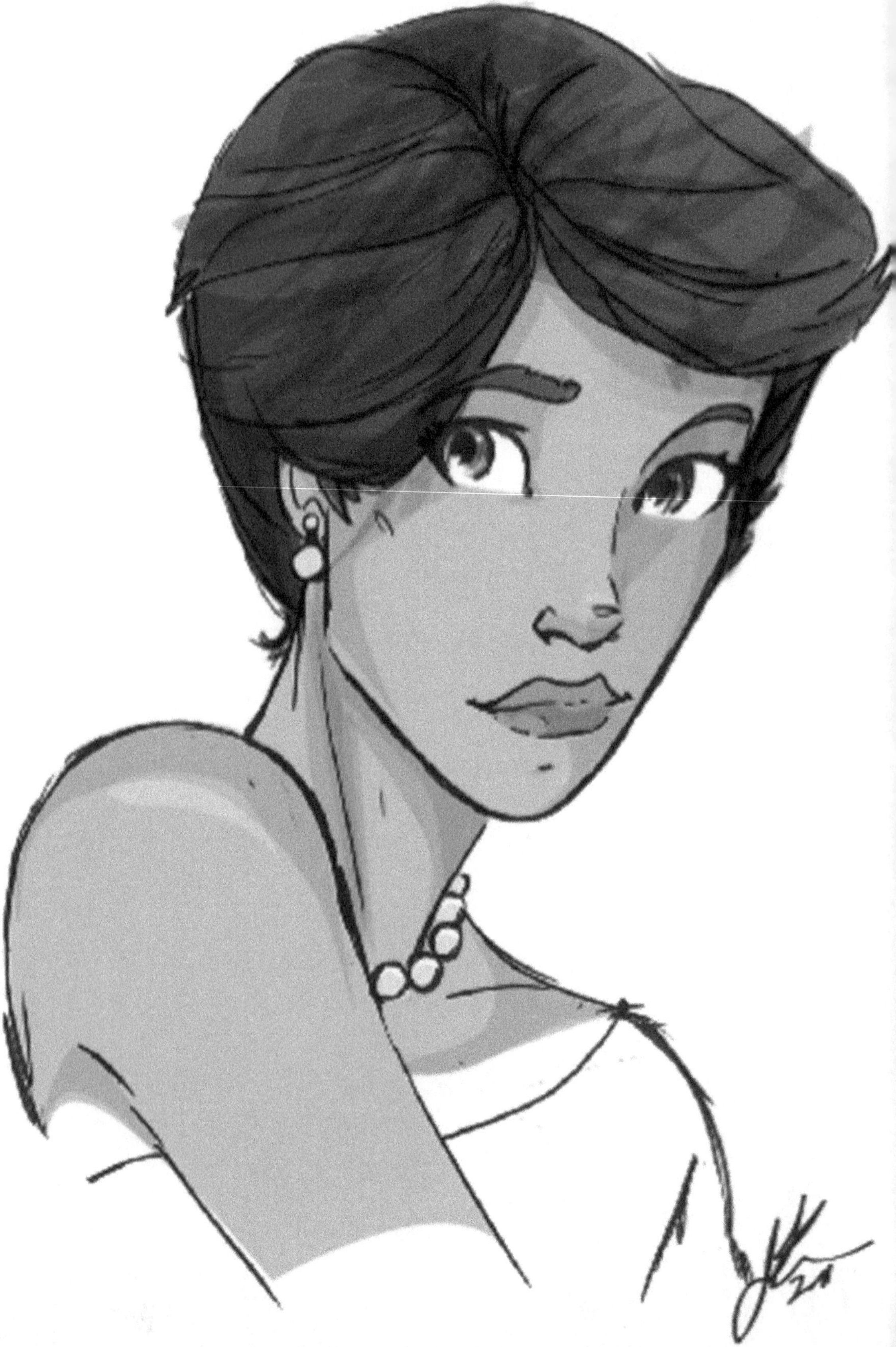

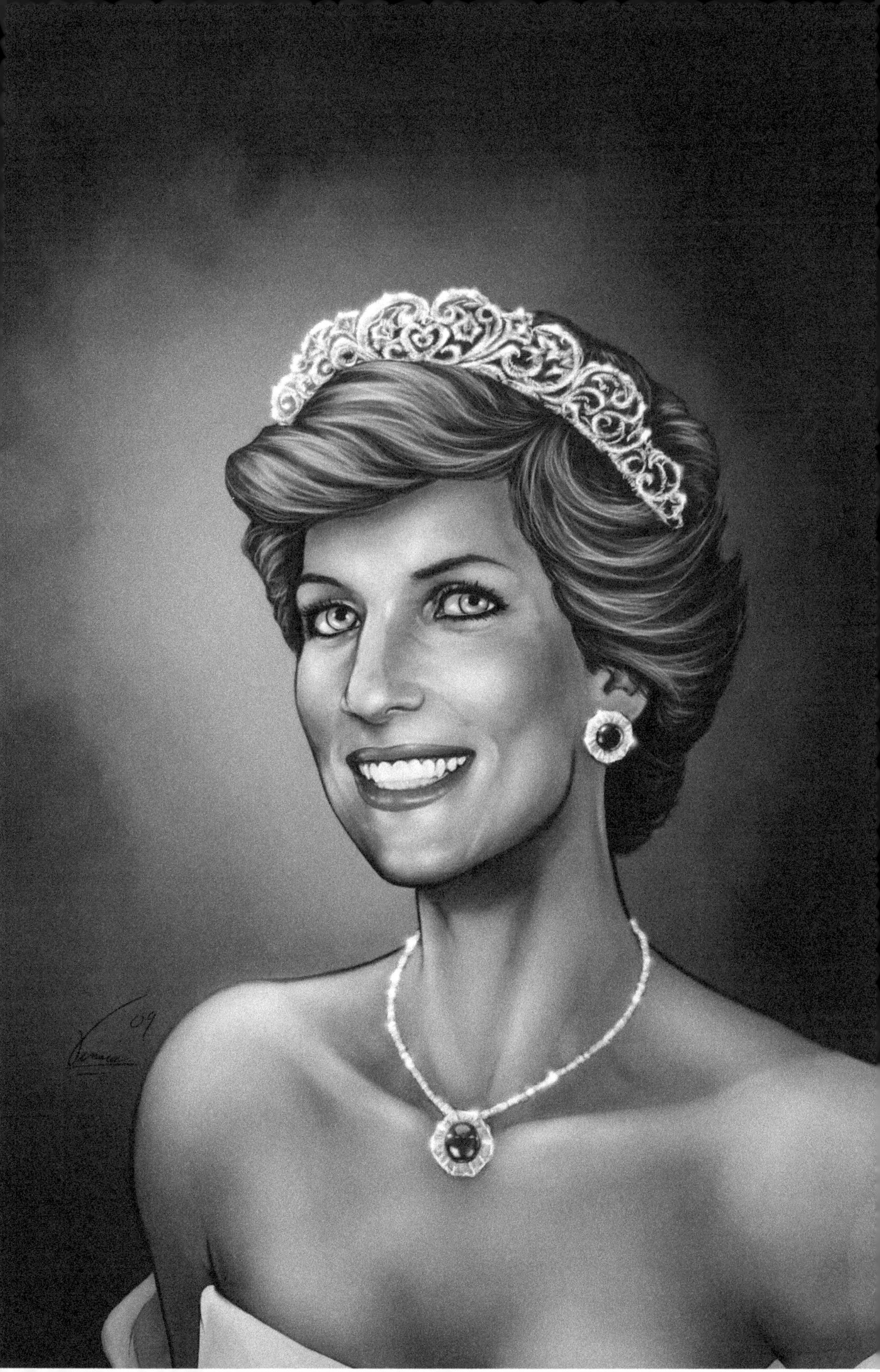

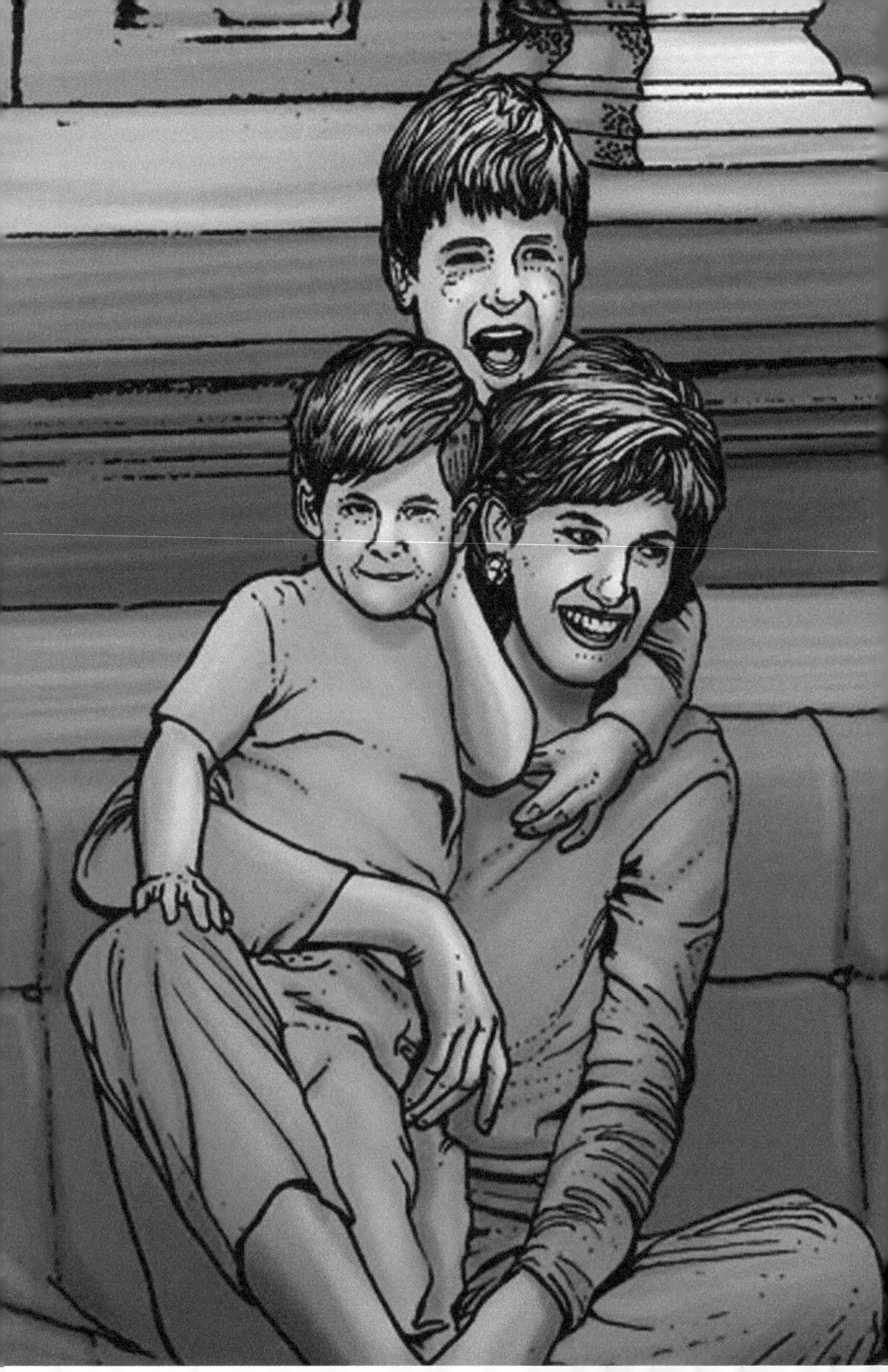

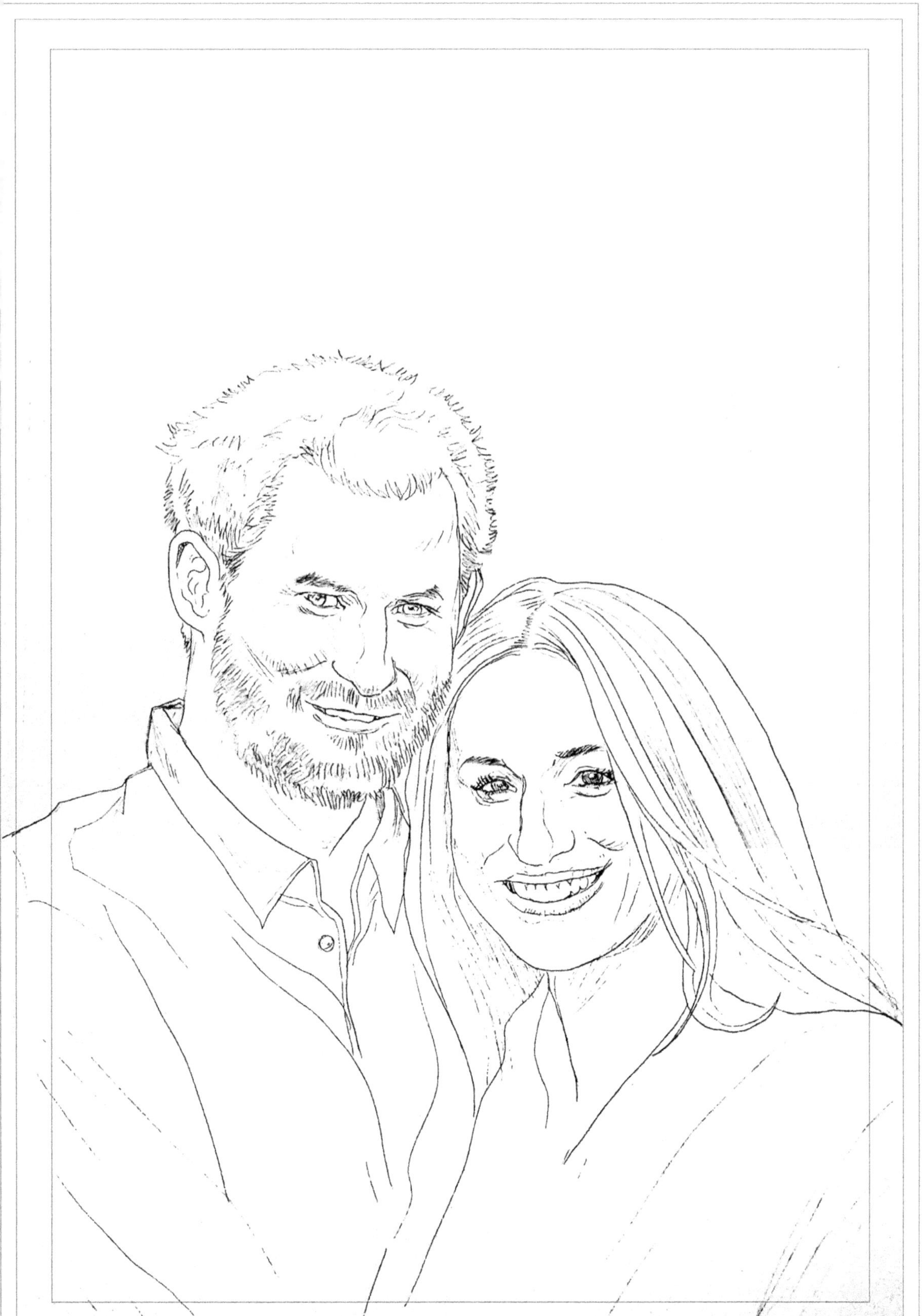

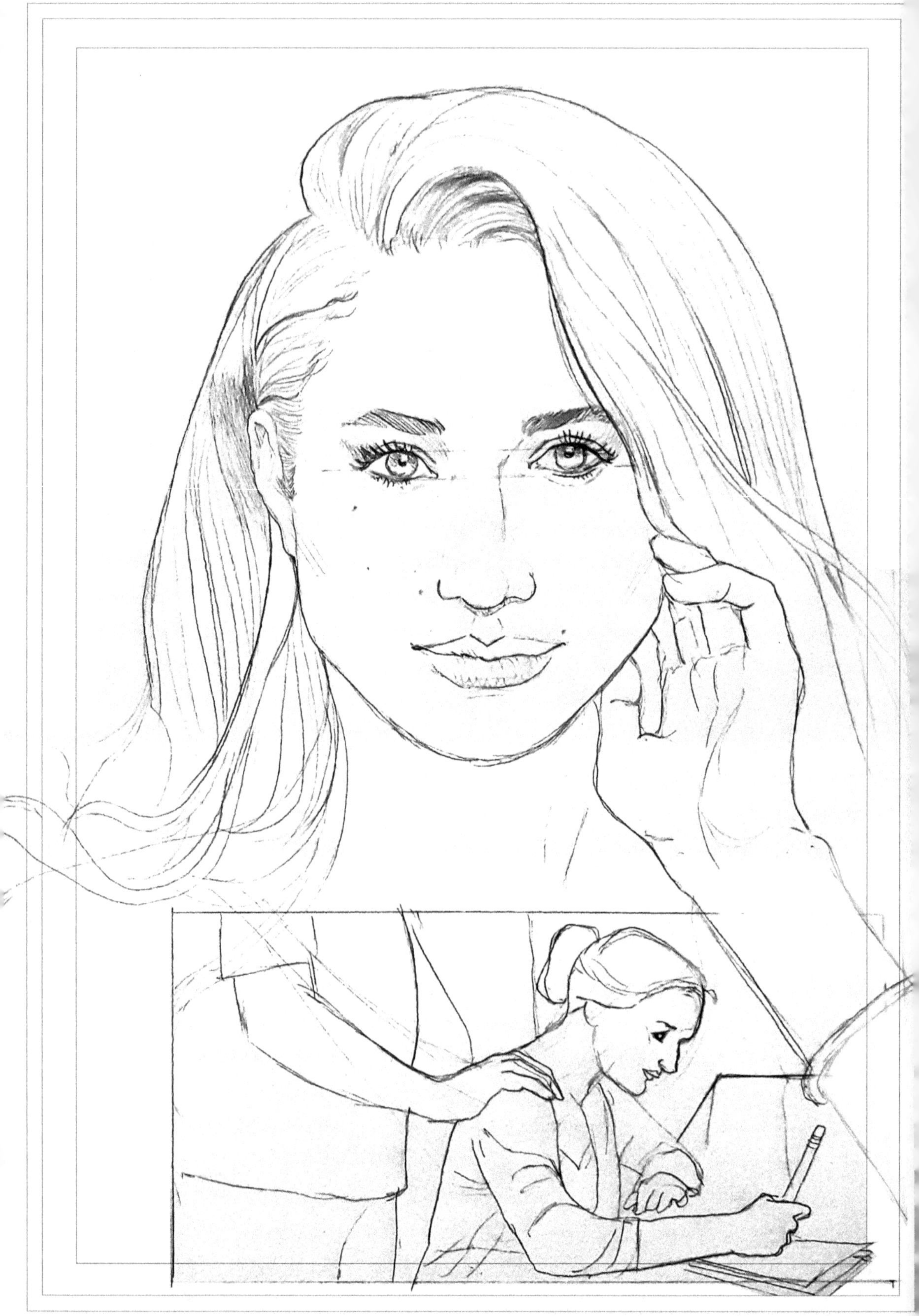

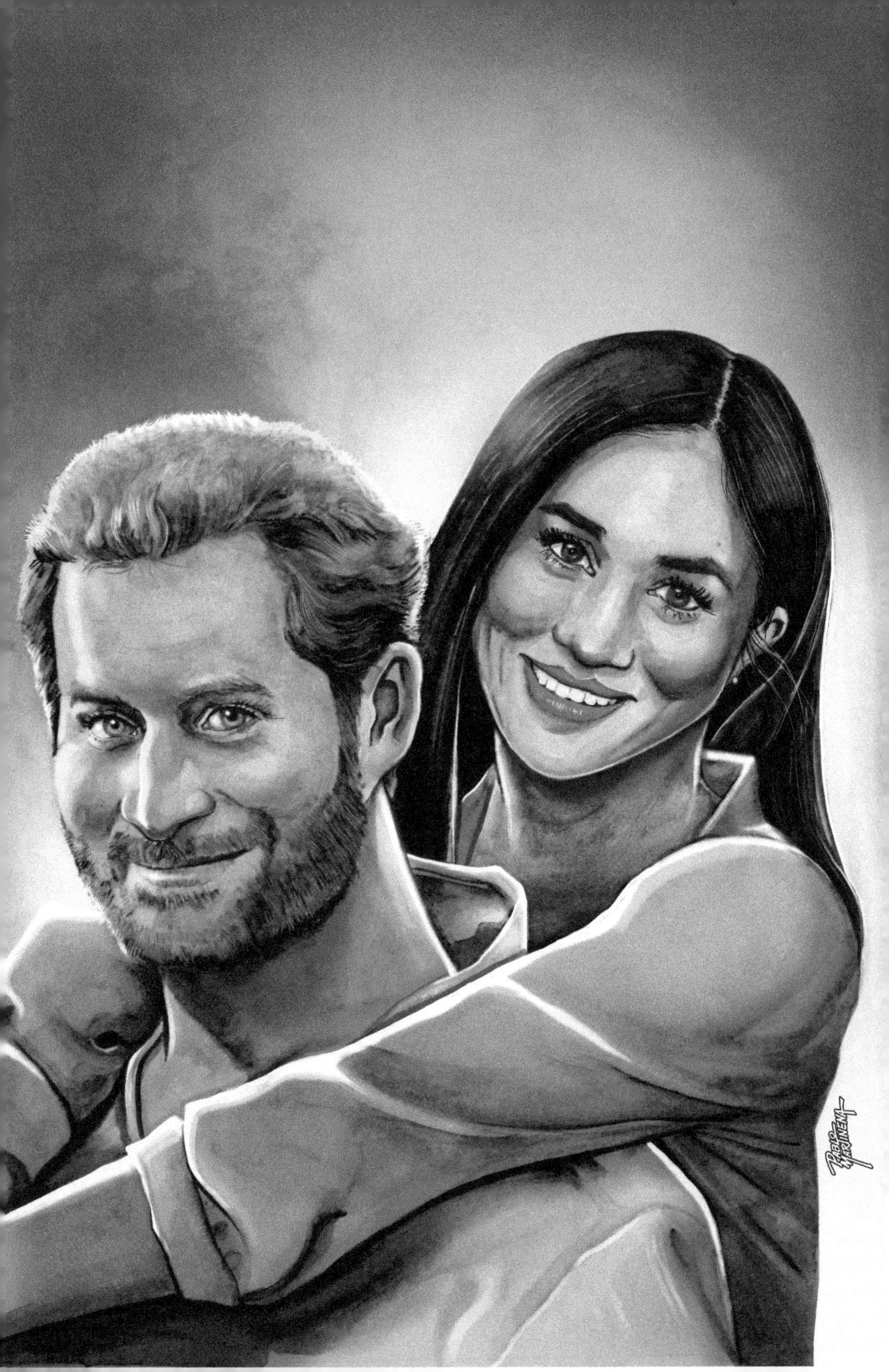

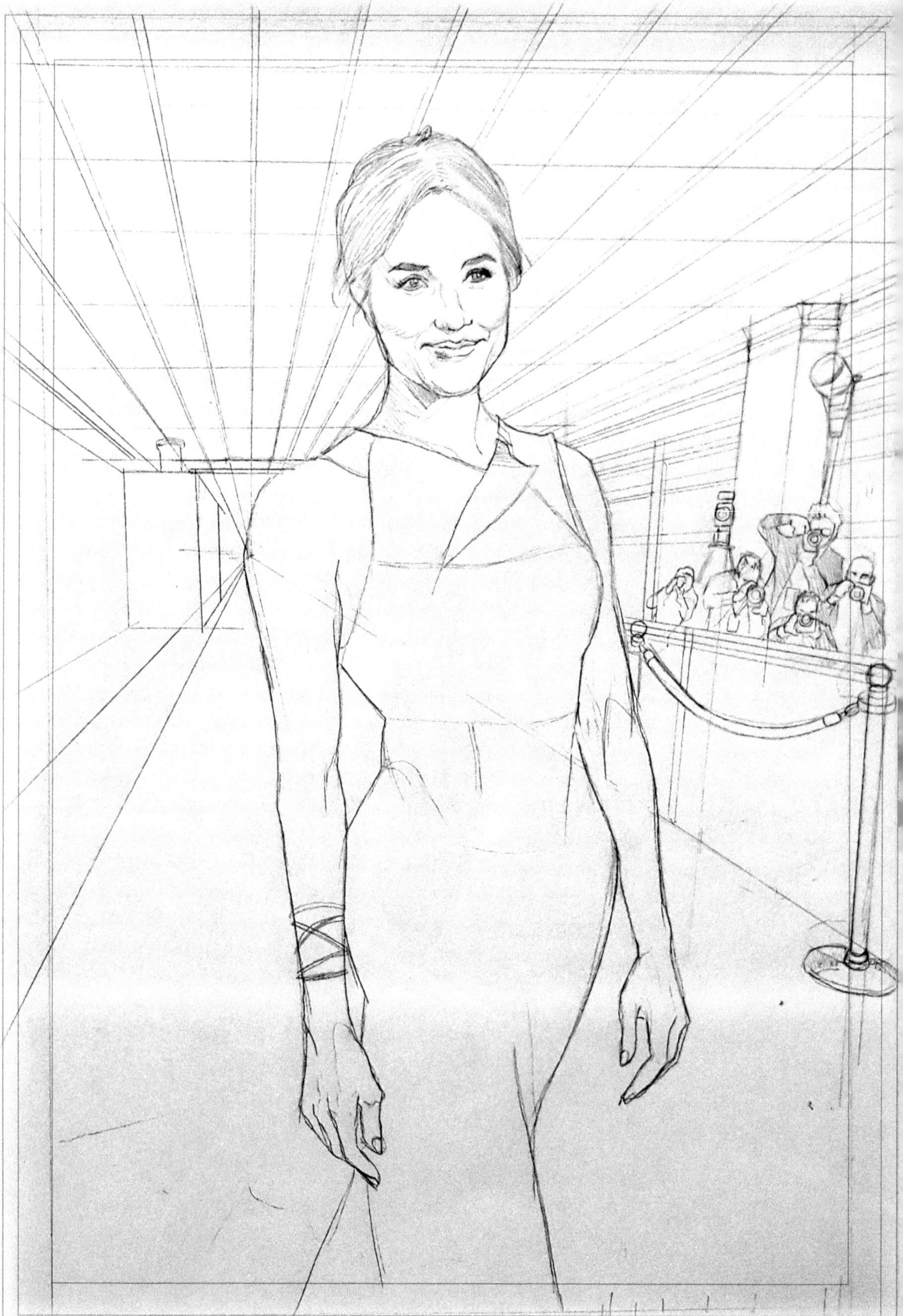

TIDALWAVE COMICS

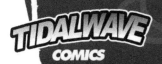

Michael L. Frizell — Writer

Pablo Martinena, Joe Phillips & Justin Currie — Art

Darren G. Davis — Editor

Benjamin Glibert — Letterer

Pablo Martinena — Cover

Graphic novel cover: Joey Mason

Darren G. Davis
Publisher

Maggie Jessup
Publicity

Susan Ferris
Entertainment Manager

TIDALWAVE PRODUCTIONS

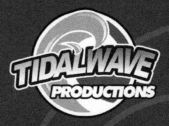

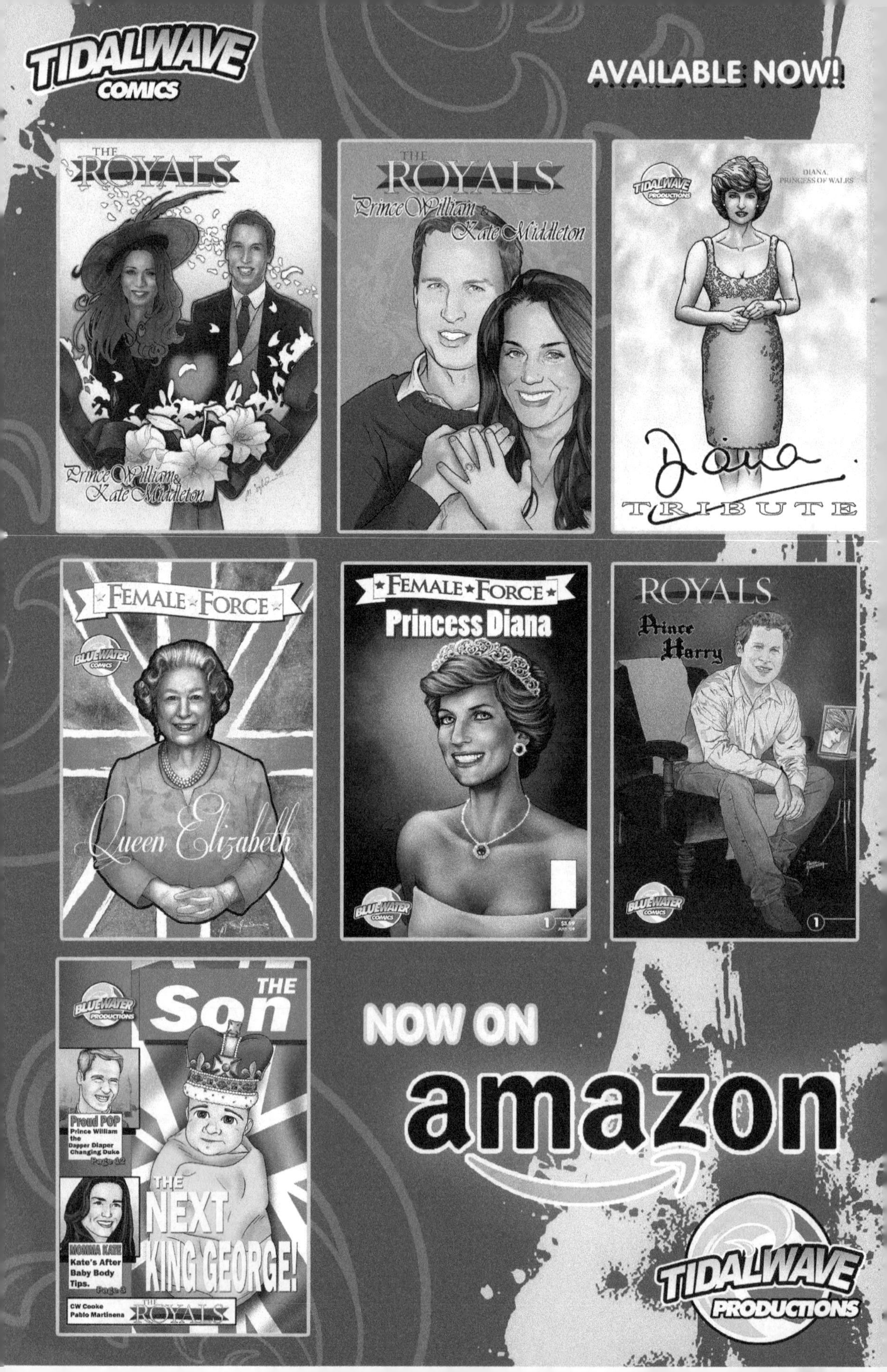
TIDALWAVE COMICS
AVAILABLE NOW!
THE ROYALS
Prince William & Kate Middleton
THE ROYALS
Prince William & Kate Middleton
TIDALWAVE PRODUCTIONS
DIANA, PRINCESS OF WALES
Diana
TRIBUTE
FEMALE FORCE
BLUEWATER COMICS
Queen Elizabeth
FEMALE FORCE
Princess Diana
BLUEWATER COMICS
ROYALS
Prince Harry
BLUEWATER COMICS
BLUEWATER PRODUCTIONS
THE Son
Proud POP
Prince William the Dapper Diaper Changing Duke
Page 12
MOMMA KATE
Kate's After Baby Body Tips.
Page 8
THE NEXT KING GEORGE!
CW Cooke
Pablo Martinena
THE ROYALS
NOW ON
amazon
TIDALWAVE PRODUCTIONS

CPSIA information can be obtained
at www.ICGtesting.com
Printed in the USA
LVHW06*1627100418
572941LV00004B/32/P

9 781948 724791